VOLUME 2

GROKKING
— THE —
JAVA INTERVIEW

JAVINPAUL @JAVINPAUL

GROKKING THE JAVA INTERVIEW

PREFACE

Welcome to the second volume of "Grokking the Java Interview." This book is a continuation of the first volume, which received an overwhelming response from readers. Based on your feedback and suggestions, we have brought to you this new edition, covering more advanced topics.

In this book, we have included topics such as class loader, Enum, String, HashMap, ConcurrentHashMap, Date and Time, Web Services, NIO, Socket Programming, Inheritance, Abstract class, and Interface. These topics are essential for any Java developer to master to ace their interviews.

We understand that Java interviews can be challenging, and preparing for them can be overwhelming. Our aim with this book is to help you grok the topics in-depth and ace your interviews with confidence.

In this book, we have provided a comprehensive explanation of each topic along with practical examples, code snippets, and interview questions to help you prepare for your interviews. We have also included a dedicated section for frequently asked interview questions to help you assess your preparation.

We hope that this book will be a valuable resource in your Java interview preparation journey. Let's get started and grok the Java interview together!

| CONTENTS

PREFACE

Welcome to the second volume of "Grokking the Java Interview." This book is a continuation of the first volume, which received an overwhelming response from readers. Based on your feedback and suggestions, we have brought to you this new edition, covering more advanced topics.

In this book, we have included topics such as class loader, Enum, String, HashMap, ConcurrentHashMap, Date and Time, Web Services, NIO, Socket Programming, Inheritance, Abstract class, and Interface. These topics are essential for any Java developer to master to ace their interviews.

We understand that Java interviews can be challenging, and preparing for them can be overwhelming. Our aim with this book is to help you grok the topics in-depth and ace your interviews with confidence.

In this book, we have provided a comprehensive explanation of each topic along with practical examples, code snippets, and interview questions to help you prepare for your interviews. We have also included a dedicated section for frequently asked interview questions to help you assess your preparation.

We hope that this book will be a valuable resource in your Java interview preparation journey. Let's get started and grok the Java interview together!

CONTENTS

CHAPTER 4: Advanced Java ClassLoader Interview Questions.....32

CHAPTER 5: Java Enum Interview Questions.................................39

CHAPTER 8: Java ConcurrentHashMap Interview Questions 69

CHAPTER 9: Java Date, Time, and Calendar Interview Questions . 76

CHAPTER 12: Java Web Service Interview Questions 106

CHAPTER 13: Java Exception and Error Interview Questions 116

CHAPTER 15: Technical Core Java Interview Questions............145

CHAPTER 1:
JAVA STRING INTERVIEW QUESTIONS

Hello Java Programmers, if you are preparing for a Java developer interview and want to refresh your knowledge about the String class in Java, you have come to the right place. In this chapter, I will share 35 Java String Questions for Interviews. The String class and concept are essential in Java. There is not a single Java program out there that does not use String objects, and that's why it's also crucial from the interview point of view. In this chapter, I will share 35 String-based questions from different Java interviews.

This list of Java String questions includes questions on `java.lang.String` class as well as a string as data structure like some coding questions.

You can use this list to refresh your knowledge about String in Java and prepare for your following Java interview.

35 Java String Concept Interview Questions and Answers

Here is the list of 35 Java Interview questions based on concepts about the String class in Java. You can also review this question to improve your knowledge about this key Java class.

Question 1

Why is String final in Java?

There are a couple of reasons for this, e.g., String pool, Caching, and Performance, but Security is probably the most important reason. Given String is used in sensitive places like specifying the host and port details, locking it for modification prevents many Security related risks. It's one of the popular Java interview questions.

Question 2

How does the substring method work in Java?

This returns a substring of a specified range from the original String on which it is called. It returns a new String object because String is immutable and can't be changed. However, prior to Java 7, it also held the reference of the original array, which can prevent it from collecting garbage and causing a memory leak, which is not ratified.

Question 3

What is the String pool in Java? What is the difference in the String pool between Java 6 and 7?

It's a pool of cached String objects to minimize the number of String instances and improve performance by sharing the same instance with multiple clients and reducing garbage collection. Prior to Java 7, the String pool was located on meta-space where class metadata was stored, but from JDK 7 onwards, it's moved into heap space.

Question 4

What is the difference between "ABC".equals(str) and str?equals("ABC"), where an str is a String object?

Though both look similar and return the same result if str is equal to "ABC," the real difference comes when the given String is null, i.e., `str = null`. In that case, the first code snippet will return false, while the second code snippet will throw `NullPointerException`.

This is one of the tricky Java questions, and if a candidate can answer this, then he has good knowledge of Java fundamentals. It's also one of the several weird tricks to avoid NullPointerException.

Question 5

Difference between str1 == str2 and str1.equals(str2)?

The critical difference is that the first one uses the `==` operator, which makes a reference-based comparison, while the second one uses the `equals()` method, which makes a content-based comparison. Since the String class overrides `equals()` to perform character-based comparison

The first will return true only if both str1 and str2 point to the same object, but the second one will return true if str1 and str2 have the same content, even if they are different objects.

Question 6

When you execute String str = new String("abcd")? how many String objects are created?

This is another tricky Java interview question, as many Java developers will answer just one, but that's not true. There are two String objects created here. The first String object is created by String literal "abcd," and the second one is created by `new String()`. If you are not sure about how

Question 7

What does the intern() method of the String class do?

The intern() method of the String class puts the String on which it has called into the String pool like `str.intern()` will put the String str into the pool. Once the String is in the pool, it can be reused and improve performance.

Question 8

How do you split comma-separated String in Java?

You can use either the StringTokenizer or the split() method of `java.lang.String` class to split a comma-separated String. The `split()` method is better because it also expects a regular expression and returns an array of String which you can use or pass to a function.

Question 9

What is the difference between String and StringBuffer in Java?

The key difference between String and StringBuffer is that String is Immutable while StringBuffer is mutable, which means you can change the content of a StringBuffer without creating separate String objects. If you are creating string programmatically, consider using `StringBuffer` for better performance as it puts less pressure on Garbage Collector by reducing the number of temporary objects.

Question 10

What is the difference between StringBuffer and StringBuilder in Java?

Now, this is interesting because both StringBuffer and StringBuilder represent mutable String. This is also asked a follow-up question to the previous question.

Anyway, the real difference is that methods of StringBuffer like `append()` are **synchronized**, hence **slow**, while those of StringBuilder is **not synchronized**, hence **fast**.

Otherwise, StringBuilder is just a copy of StringBuffer, and you can see that in the Javadoc of the `StringBuilder` class as well.

Question 11

Write a program to reverse a String in Java without using StringBuffer.

This is a common coding problem from Java interviews. You can use recursion or iteration to solve this problem.

Here's a simple program to reverse a String in Java without using StringBuffer:

```java
public class StringReverse {

    public static void main(String[] args) {
        String str = "Hello, world!";
        String reversedStr = reverse(str);
        System.out.println("Reversed String: " +
reversedStr);
    }

    public static String reverse(String str) {
        char[] chars = str.toCharArray();
        int left = 0;
        int right = chars.length - 1;

        while (left < right) {
            char temp = chars[left];
            chars[left] = chars[right];
            chars[right] = temp;
            left++;
            right--;
        }

        return new String(chars);
    }
}
```

In this program, we have first defined a **reverse()** method that takes a String as input and returns the reversed String. We then convert the input String to a character array using the **toCharArray()** method.

We then use two pointers, **left** and **right**, to traverse the character array from both ends. We swap the characters at **left** and **right** positions until we reach the middle of the array.

Finally, we return the reversed String by creating a new String object from the character array using the **String(char[] chars)** constructor.

Question 12

Write a program to replace a character from a given one in Java.

This is another coding problem based on String, but it doesn't specify whether you can use String API. If not, then you can use the replace method of String to solve this problem.

Here's a Java program to replace a character from a given String:

```java
import java.util.Scanner;

public class ReplaceChar {

    public static void main(String[] args) {
        Scanner input = new Scanner(System.in);
        System.out.println("Enter a string: ");
        String str = input.nextLine();
        System.out.println("Enter the character to replace: ");
        char oldChar = input.next().charAt(0);
        System.out.println("Enter the new character: ");
        char newChar = input.next().charAt(0);
        String newStr = replaceChar(str, oldChar, newChar);
        System.out.println("Modified string: " + newStr);
    }

    public static String replaceChar(String str, char oldChar, char newChar) {
        char[] charArray = str.toCharArray();
        for (int i = 0; i < charArray.length; i++) {
            if (charArray[i] == oldChar) {
                charArray[i] = newChar;
            }
        }
        return new String(charArray);
    }
}
```

In this program, we first take the input String from the user using a Scanner object. Then we take the character to be replaced and the new character as input. The **replaceChar()** method takes the input String, old character, and new character as input and return a String where the old character is replaced with a new character.

Question 13

Can you write a Java program to count the occurrence of a given character in String?

This problem requires using HashMap for string characters as keys and their count as values. Once you know this trick, you can easily solve such string coding problems. Just convert String to character array and then loop through the array. For each character, store the character as a key and the value as 1 in HashMap. If the key or character already exists, then increase the count by 1.

here's an example Java program to count the occurrence of a given character in a String:

```
public class CharacterCount {
    public static int countOccurrences(String str, char
ch) {
        int count = 0;
        for (int i = 0; i < str.length(); i++) {
            if (str.charAt(i) == ch) {
                count++;
            }
        }
        return count;
    }
}
```

This program defines a `countOccurrences()` method that takes a String and a character as input, and returns the number of times the character appears in the String. The main() method demonstrates how to use the `countOccurrences()` method to count the number of occurrences of the letter 'l' in the String "Hello World".

When you run this program you will see following output:

```
Number of occurrences of '1' in "Hello World": 3
```

Question 14

Why is a char array better than a String for storing sensitive information?

This is one of the trick questions from Java interviews. The reason is that **because String is immutable, they are cached in memory,** and there is a good chance that they will remain in memory for a longer duration posing a possible threat, while character array gives you the option to erase data once they are used. This is the primary reason, but there are some more subtle reasons.

Question 15

How to check if a String contains only numeric digits?

This is one of the simple problem to solve. You can either use a regular expression to check if a string contains only numbers, or you can convert it to a character array and then check the ASCII value of those characters to see if they are in the range of numbers. For example, You can use the **matches()** method in Java with a regular expression to check if a **String** contains only numeric digits as shown below:

```
public static boolean containsOnlyDigits(String str) {
    return str.matches("\\d+");
}
```

This method takes a **String** as input and returns a boolean indicating whether the **String** contains only numeric digits or not. The regular expression \\d+ matches one or more digits. The **matches()** method returns true if the **String** matches the regular expression and false otherwise.

Question 16

Can you write a program to check if a String is a palindrome in Java?

If you don't know, *a string is said to be a palindrome if it's equal to its reverse.* In order to check if a given String is a palindrome or not, you need to first reverse it and then compare the reversed string with the original string. If they are equal, the given String is a palindrome. If you remember, we have seen questions about reversing a string, you can either use that technique to reverse a string, or you can use convert the String to StringBuffer and use its reverse() method to reverse the given string.

Here's a Java program to check if a given string is a palindrome or not:

```java
import java.util.Scanner;

public class Palindrome {

    public static void main(String[] args) {
        Scanner sc = new Scanner(System.in);
        System.out.print("Enter a string: ");
        String str = sc.nextLine();
        if(isPalindrome(str)){
            System.out.println(str + " is a palindrome.");
        } else {
            System.out.println(str + " is not a
palindrome.");
        }
    }

    public static boolean isPalindrome(String str){
        int len = str.length();
        for(int i=0; i<len/2; i++){
            if(str.charAt(i) != str.charAt(len-i-1)){
                return false;
            }
        }
        return true;
    }
}
```

In the above program, we first take input string from the user using Scanner. Then, we check if the string is palindrome or not using **isPalindrome()** method. This method takes a string as input and returns a boolean value **true** if the string is a palindrome; otherwise **false**. To check if the string is palindrome, we compare the characters from start and end of the string and return **false** as soon as we find a mismatch. If we reach the middle of the string without finding any mismatch, we return **true**.

Question 17

How to format String in Java?

You can use the `format()` method of the `java.lang.String` class to format a given String in Java. If you just want to print the formatted String, you can also use the `System.out.printf()` method, which prints the formatted string to the console.

Question 18

How to convert Enum to String in Java?

Similar to any Java object, you can also use the `toString()` method to convert an Enum to a String in Java. The Enum class provides a `toString()` method which can be overridden by your Enum implementations.

Question 19

How to convert String to Date in Java?

Prior to Java 8, you could use DateFormat or SimpleDateFormat class to convert a String to Date In Java or vice-versa. From Java 8 onwards, when you use the new Date and Time API, you can also use the DateTimeFormatter class to convert String to `LocalDate`, `LocalTime`, or `LocalDateTime` class in Java.

Question 20

Is String thread-safe in Java? Why?

Yes, String is thread-safe because it's Immutable. All Immutable objects are thread-safe because once they are created, they can't be modified. Hence is no issue with respect to multiple threads accessing them.

Question 21

Can we use String as the HashMap key in Java?

Yes, we can use String as a key in HashMap because it implements the `equals()` and `hashcode()` method, which is required for an object to be used as a key in `HashMap`.

Question 22

How to check if a String is empty in Java?

There are many ways to check if a String is empty in Java, e.g., **you can check its length**. If the length of the String is zero, then it's empty. Otherwise, you can also use the `isEmpty()` method, which returns true if the String is empty. Though you need to be careful with requirements, e.g., a String may contain a whitespace that will look empty, but the length will not be zero. So, it depends upon your requirements.

Question 23

How to convert String to int in Java?

There are many ways to convert the String to the int primitive in Java, but the best way is by using `Integer.parseInt()` method. This method parses the given string and returns a primitive int value. If you need a wrapper class Integer object, you can use `Integer.valueOf()` method. Although it internally uses the `parseInt()` method, it caches frequently used Integer values, e.g., -128 to 127, which can reduce temporary objects.

Question 24

How does String concatenation using the + operator work in Java?

The + operator can be used to concatenate two Strings in Java. This is the only operator that is overloaded, i.e., it can be used two add numbers as well as to concatenate String. Internally, the concatenation is done by using `StringBuffer`, or StringBuilder `append()` method, depending upon which version of Java you are using.

Question 25

Can we use String in switch case in Java?

Yes, after the JDK 7 release, you can use the String in the switch case in Java. Earlier, it wasn't possible, but now it's possible.

Question 26

What is the String enum pattern in Java?

This is a common pattern to declare String constants inside an enum. For example, days of the Week can be declared as Enum so that you can use them as Enum instead of String.

Question 27

Write a Java program to print all permutations of a String.

This is also one of the most popular string coding problems, which can be easily solved using recursion, provided you know the permutations.

Here is a Java program to print all permutations of a String using recursion:

```java
import java.util.*;

public class StringPermutations {

    public static void main(String[] args) {
        String str = "ABC";
```

```java
        List<String> permutations =
getPermutations(str);
        System.out.println("Permutations of " + str + ":
" + permutations);
    }

    public static List<String> getPermutations(String
str) {
        List<String> permutations = new ArrayList<>();
        if (str == null || str.length() == 0) {
            return permutations;
        }
        getPermutations(str.toCharArray(), 0,
permutations);
        return permutations;
    }

    private static void getPermutations(char[] str, int
index, List<String> permutations) {
        if (index == str.length - 1) {
            permutations.add(new String(str));
        } else {
            for (int i = index; i < str.length; i++) {
                swap(str, index, i);
                getPermutations(str, index + 1,
permutations);
                swap(str, index, i);
            }
        }
    }

    private static void swap(char[] str, int i, int j) {
        char temp = str[i];
        str[i] = str[j];
        str[j] = temp;
    }
}
```

This program uses recursion to generate all possible permutations of the input String. It first checks if the String is null or empty, and if so, returns an empty list. Otherwise, it calls a helper function that takes in the String as a character array, an index representing the current position in the array, and a list to store the permutations.

If the index is at the end of the array, the function adds the current permutation to the list. Otherwise, it swaps the current character with every character to its right and recursively generates permutations for the remaining characters. After each recursive call, it swaps the characters back to their original positions to backtrack and generate the next permutation.

Question 28

What is the difference between String in C and Java?

Even though both C and Java String is backed by character array, C String is a NULL-terminated character array while Java String is an object. This means you can call methods on Java String, e.g., `length`, `toUpperCase`, `toLowerCase`, `substring`, etc.

Question 29

How to convert String to double in Java?

Similar to `Integer.parseInt()` method, which is used to convert a String to int, you can also use the `Double.parseDouble()` method to convert a String to a double primitive value.

Question 30

How to convert String to long in Java?

It's similar to converting String to int or String to double in Java. All you need to do is just use the `parseLong()` method of the Long class. This method returns a primitive long value. Even though you can use the `Long.valueOf()` method, which can be used to convert String to Long but it returns a Long object. Hence you would need to use auto-boxing to convert the wrapper object to a primitive value.

Question 31

What is the difference between the format() and printf() methods in Java?

Even though both methods can be used to format Strings and they have the same rules, the key difference is that `format()` method returns a formatted String while the `printf()` method prints a formatted String to the console. So, if you need a formatted String, use the format method, and if you want to print, then use the `printf()` method.

Question 32

How do you append a leading zero to a numeric String?

You can use the `format()` method of String to append leading zeros to a numeric String in Java.

Question 33

How to remove white space from String in Java?

You can use the `trim()` method to remove white space from String in Java. It's similar to SQL Servers `LTRIM()` and `RTRIM()` methods.

Question 34

How to check if two Strings are Anagram in Java?

There are multiple ways to solve this problem. One way is to sort both strings and then compare them. This way, all characters will come into the same place, and if Strings are anagrams, then they will be equal to each other.

Here's a Java program to check if two strings are anagrams or not:

```java
import java.util.Arrays;

public class AnagramChecker {

    public static boolean areAnagrams(String str1,
String str2) {
        // If lengths of both strings are not equal,
they cannot be anagrams
        if (str1.length() != str2.length()) {
            return false;
        }

        // Convert strings to char arrays, sort them,
and compare
        char[] arr1 = str1.toCharArray();
        char[] arr2 = str2.toCharArray();
        Arrays.sort(arr1);
        Arrays.sort(arr2);
        return Arrays.equals(arr1, arr2);
    }

    public static void main(String[] args) {
        String str1 = "listen";
        String str2 = "silent";

        if (areAnagrams(str1, str2)) {
            System.out.println(str1 + " and " + str2 + "
are anagrams.");
        } else {
            System.out.println(str1 + " and " + str2 + "
are not anagrams.");
        }
    }
}
```

The program takes two strings as input and returns **true** if they are anagrams of each other and **false** otherwise. It first checks if the lengths of the strings are equal since if they're not, they cannot be anagrams. Then it converts both strings to char arrays, sorts them, and checks if they are equal using the **Arrays.equals()** method. If the char arrays are equal, the strings are anagrams

Question 35

What is character encoding? What is the difference between UTF-8 and UTF-16?

Character encoding is an algorithm that represents a character using bytes. The UTF-8 character encoding uses 1 byte or 8 bits to represent a character of UTF-16 uses 2 bytes or 16 bits to represent a character. They come into the picture when you convert raw bytes to characters or strings in Java.

That's all about the **top 35 Java String Interview Questions**. These questions are not only good for preparing for Java job interviews but also expand your knowledge about String in Java, one of the key classes of JDKD. Even after programming in Java for more than 20 years, I still discover things about core classes that I should have known earlier. Truly, there is so much to learn in Java.

CHAPTER 2:
ABSTRACT CLASS AND INTERFACE QUESTIONS

A bstract class and interface are very popular in any object-oriented programming language or Java interview, and there are always one or more questions from this. The interface is more common because of its popularity among designers, but questions from abstract classes also pop up occasionally. Interview questions from the abstract class are more common on the junior level or under two years of experience for Java programmers, while interface-related questions are mostly asked in senior-level Java interviews, e.g., 4 or 6 years of experience. They are also mostly asked along with other Java design pattern questions, like the **Decorator pattern** or Factory pattern. In this chapter, we will see a mix of these interview questions from abstract class and interface. All questions have been asked in various Java interviews, and the difficulty level for these questions is easy for most Java developers.

It's mostly fact-based questions, but some questions, *like the difference between abstract class and interface in Java* and *when to prefer abstract class over the interface,* can be tricky and require deep knowledge of object-oriented programming and Java.

10 Frequently asked Abstract class and Interface questions in Java

Here is my list of questions. This explains rules related to abstract classes and shares some tricky questions about using abstract classes and interfaces. If you have asked any question on this topic, which you don't see in this list, then please share with us as a comment

Question 1

Can abstract classes have constructors in Java?

Yes, an abstract class can declare and define a constructor in Java. Since you cannot create an instance of an abstract class, a constructor can only be called during constructor chaining, i.e., when you create an instance of the concrete implementation class.

Now some interviewers ask what the purpose of a constructor is if you can not instantiate an abstract class. Well, it can still be used to initialize common variables, declared inside an abstract class and used by various implementations.

Also, the compiler will add a default no-argument constructor in an abstract class even if you don't provide any constructor. Without that, your subclass will not compile since the first statement in any constructor implicitly calls `super ()`, the default superclass constructor in Java.

Question 2

Can abstract class implement the interface in Java? Do they require to implement all methods?

Yes, an abstract class can implement an interface using the `implements` keyword. Since they are abstract, they don't need to implement all methods. It's good practice to provide an abstract base class and an interface to declare Type.

One example of this is `java.util.List` interface and corresponding `java.util.AbstractList` abstract class.

Since `AbstractList` implements all common methods, concrete implementations like LinkedList and ArrayList are free from the burden of implementing all methods had they implemented the `List` interface directly.

It's the best of both worlds. You can get the advantage of an interface for declaring the type and flexibility of abstract classes to implement common behavior in one place. Effective Java has a nice chapter on how to use interface and abstract classes in Java, which is worth reading.

Question 3

Can an abstract class be final in Java?

No, an abstract class can not be final in Java. Making them final will stop the abstract class from being extended, which is the only way to use an abstract class. They are also opposite each other. The `abstract` keyword enforces extending a class for using it. On the other hand, the final keyword prevents a class from being extended.

In real-world also, abstract signifies incompleteness, while final is used to demonstrate completeness. The bottom line is you can not make your class `abstract` and `final` in Java; at the same time, it's a compile-time error.

Question 4

Can abstract classes have static methods in Java?

Yes, an abstract class can declare and define static methods. Nothing prevents doing that. But, you must follow guidelines for making a method static in Java, as it's not welcomed in an object-oriented design because static methods can not be overridden in Java. It's very rare you see static methods inside an abstract class, but as I said, if you have a very good reason for doing it, then nothing stops you.

Question 5

Can you create an instance of an abstract class?

No, you can not create instances of abstract classes in Java. They are incomplete. Even though, if your abstract class doesn't contain any abstract method, you can not create an instance of it. By making a class `abstract`, you told the compiler that it's incomplete and should not be instantiated. Java compiler will throw an error when a code tries to instantiate an abstract class.

Question 6

Is it necessary for an abstract class to have an abstract method?

No, it's not mandatory for an abstract class to have any abstract method. You can make a class abstract in Java by just using the `abstract` keyword in the class declaration. The compiler will enforce all structural restrictions applied to an abstract class, like, not allowing to create of any instance.

By the way, it's debatable whether you should have an abstract method inside the abstract class or interface. In my opinion, the abstract class should have abstract methods because that's the first thing programmer assumes when he sees that class. That would also go nicely along with the principle of least surprise.

Question 7

What is the difference between abstract class and interface in Java?

This is the most important and one of the classic Java Interview questions. I don't know how often I have seen this question at all levels of Java interviews. One reason which makes this question interesting is the ability to produce examples.

It's easy to answer questions on core OOP concepts like Abstraction, Encapsulation, Polymorphism, and Inheritance, but when it comes to subtle points like this, a candidate more often fumbles. You can see this post for all syntactical differences between abstract class and interface, but it deserves a post on its own.

Question 8

When do you favor abstract classes over interface?

This is the follow-up to previous interview questions on abstract class and interface. If you know the syntactical difference, you can answer this question quite easily, as they are the ones that drive the decision. Since adding a new method to a published interface is almost impossible, it's better to use an abstract class when evolution is a concern.

Abstract class in Java evolves better than the interface. Similarly, if you have too many methods inside the interface, you create pain for all its implementation; consider providing an abstract class for default implementation. This is the pattern followed in the Java collection package. You can see `AbstractList` provides a default implementation for the `List` interface.

Question 9

What is the abstract method in Java?

An abstract method is a method without a body. You just declare the method without defining it and use `abstract` keywords in the method declaration. All methods declared inside Java Interface are, by default, abstract. Here is an example of an abstract method in Java:

```java
public void abstract printVersion();
```

To implement this method, you need to extend the abstract class and override this method.

Question 10

Can an abstract class contain the main method in Java?

Yes, an abstract class can contain the `main()` method. It is just another static method; you can execute the Abstract class with the main method until you don't create any instance.

That's all on this **list of interview questions on abstract classes, interfaces, and methods in Java**. You can review these questions about the abstract class before the interview. On a different note, choosing abstract class and interface are key design decisions on object-oriented analysis and design process and should be taken by applying due diligence, of course, if you want to write flexible systems. From JDK 8 onward, there are also a lot of addition in core Java interfaces like Collecitona and Map because its now possible to add new methods without breaking all the implementations of an interface, thanks to default or defender methods.

CHAPTER 3:
JAVA INHERITANCE INTERVIEW QUESTIONS

In this chapter, I am going to share some **frequently asked Inheritance-based Java Interview questions and answers.** Inheritance is one of the most important Object-oriented concepts, along with Abstraction, Encapsulation, and Polymorphism. Since most popular languages are object-oriented, like Java and C++, you will always find a couple of questions from OOP concepts, particularly from Polymorphism and Inheritance.

It's expected of Java developers to know about these OOP concepts and have an understanding of when to use them as many times. Composition is the better choice than Inheritance because of the flexibility it offers, but when it comes to leveraging polymorphism of type, you have to use Inheritance. In Java, inheritance is supported by language using `extends` and `implements` keywords.

In Java, a `class` can extend another class and implement the `interface`, but an interface can only extend other interfaces. At the same time, Java doesn't support multiple inheritances just like C++ does, but it does support multiple inheritances of type by allowing an interface to extend multiple interfaces. You will see many such Inheritance based Java questions in this article.

21 Frequently asked Java Inheritance Interview Questions and Answers

Here is my list of interview questions based on the Inheritance OOP concept asked in various Java interviews. It's very useful for beginners, freshers, and junior Java programmers. Still, intermediate Java developers can also benefit from some advanced questions shared in this article, e.g., the position of multiple inheritances in Java after JDK 1.8 release, which allows you to write code inside interface in the form of default methods or explaining Liskov substitution principle.

Question 1

What is Inheritance in Java?

Inheritance is an Object-oriented feature that allows a class to inherit behavior and data from other classes. For example, a class Car can extend the basic features of the Vehicle class by using Inheritance. One of the most intuitive examples of Inheritance in the real world is the Father-Son relationship, where Son inherits Father's property. If you don't know, Inheritance is the quick way to become rich :)

Question 2

What are the different types of Inheritance supported by Java?

Answer: Java supports single Inheritance, multi-level inheritance, and to some extent, multiple inheritances because Java allows a class to only extend another class, but an interface in Java can extend multiple inheritances.

Question 3

Why is multiple Inheritance not supported by Java?

Java was introduced after C++, and Java designers didn't want to take some C++ features, which are confusing and unnecessary. They think multiple inheritances are one of them, which doesn't justify the complexity and confusion it introduces. You can also check why multiple inheritances are not supported in Java for more reasons and discussions around this.

Question 4

Why is Inheritance used by Java Programmers?

Inheritance is used for code reuse and leveraging Polymorphism by creating a type of hierarchy. It's better to use Inheritance for type declaration, but the composition is a better option for code reuse because it's more flexible.

Question 5

How to use Inheritance in Java?

You can use Inheritance in Java by extending classes and implementing interfaces. Java provides two keywords, extends, and implements to achieve inheritance. A class derived from another class is known as a subclass, and an interface derived from another interface is called a subinterface. A class that implements an interface is known as an implementation.

Question 6

What is the syntax of Inheritance?

You can use either `extends` or `implements` keywords to implement Inheritance in Java. A `class` extends another class using `extends` keyword, an interface can extend another interface using extend keyword, and a class can implement an interface using the implements keyword in Java.

Question 7

What is the difference between Inheritance and Encapsulation?

Inheritance is an object-oriented concept that creates a parent-child relationship. It is one of the ways to reuse the code written for the parent class, but it also forms the basis of Polymorphism. On the other hand, Encapsulation is an object-oriented concept used to hide a class's internal details; e.g., HashMap encapsulates how to store elements and calculate hash values.

Question 8

What is the difference between Inheritance and Abstraction?

Abstraction is an object-oriented concept that is used to simply things by abstracting details. It helps in the design system. On the other hand, Inheritance allows code reuse. You can reuse the functionality you have already coded by using Inheritance.

Question 9

What is the difference between Polymorphism and Inheritance?

Both Polymorphism and Inheritance go hand in hand. They help each other to achieve their goal. Polymorphism allows flexibility. You can choose which code to run at runtime by overriding. See the detailed answer for more details.

Question 10

What is the difference between Composition and Inheritance in OOP?

One of the good questions is to check the candidate's object-oriented programming skills. There are several differences between Composition and Inheritance in Java, some of them are the following:

1. The Composition is more flexible because you can change the implementation at runtime by calling setXXX() method, but Inheritance cannot be changed, i.e., you cannot ask a class to implement another class at runtime.

2. The composition builds a HAS-A relationship while Inheritance builds an IS-A relationship, e.g., A Room HAS A Fan, but Mango IS-A Fruit.

3. The parent-child relationship is best represented using Inheritance, but If you just want to use the services of another class, use Composition.

Question 11

Can we override the static method in Java?

No, you cannot override a static method in Java because it's resolved at compile time. In order for overriding to work, a method should be virtual and resolved at runtime because objects are only available at runtime. This is one of the tricky Java questions where the interviewer tries to confuse you. A programmer is never sure about whether they can override or overload a static method in Java.

Question 12

Can we overload a static method in Java?

Yes, you can overload a static method in Java. Overloading has nothing to do with runtime, but the signature of each method must be different. In Java, to change the method signature, you must change either number of arguments, type of arguments, or order of arguments.

Question 13

Can we override a private method in Java?

No, you cannot override a private method in Java because the subclass does not inherit the private method in Java, which is essential for overriding. In fact, a private method is not visible to anyone outside the class, and, more importantly, a call to the private method is resolved at compile time by using Type information as opposed to runtime by using the actual object.

Question 14

What is Method Hiding in Java?

Since the static method cannot be overridden in Java, declaring the same static method in the subclass would hide the method from the superclass. It means if you call that method from the subclass, then the one in the subclass will be invoked, but if you call the same method from the superclass, then the one in the superclass will be invoked. This is known as Method Hiding in Java.

Question 15

Can a class implement more than one interface in Java?

Yes, A class can implement more than one interface in Java, e.g., A class can be both Comparable and Serializable simultaneously. This is why the interface should be best for defining Type as described in Effective Java. This feature allows one class to play a polymorphic role in the program.

Question 16

Can a class extend more than one class in Java?

No, a class can only extend just one more class in Java. Though Every class also, by default, extends the `java.lang.Object` class in Java.

Question 17

Can an interface extend more than one interface in Java?

Unlike classes, an interface can extend more than one interface in Java. There are several examples of this behavior in JDK, e.g., `java.util.List` interface extends both `Collection` and `Iterable` interface to tell that it is a Collection and allows iteration via Iterator.

Question 18

What will happen if a class extends two interfaces and they both have a method with the same name and signature?

In this case, a conflict will arise because the compiler cannot link a method call due to ambiguity. You will get a compile time error in Java.

Question 19

Can we pass an object of a subclass to a method expecting an object of the super class?

Yes, you can pass that because subclass and superclass are related by Inheritance which provides IS-A property. Banana is a Fruit, so you can pass a banana if somebody expects fruit. Now there are scenarios where you can't do, e.g., when subclass violates the Liskov Substitution principle, i.e., you cannot pass a plastic banana to someone expecting fruit :-), The eat() function will throw an exception.

Question 20

What is the Liskov substitution principle?

The Liskov substitution principle is one of the five object-oriented design principles, collectively known as SOLID principles.

This design principle is L of the SOLID acronym. The Liskov substitution principle states that in an object-oriented program, if a function or method is expecting an object of a base class, it should also work fine with a derived class object. If it cannot function properly with a derived class object, then the derived class violates the Liskov Substitution principle.

For example, suppose a method is expecting a List. In that case, you can also pass ArrayList or LinkedList, and it should work just fine because ArrayList and LinkedList both follow Liskov Substitution Principle, but the `java.sql.Date`, which is a subclass of `java.util.Date` in Java violates Liskov Substitution Principle because you cannot pass an object of `java.sql.Date` class to a method expecting an object of java.util.Date, Why? Because all time-related methods will throw `java.lang.UnsupportedOperationException`.

Another example of violating The Liskov Substitution Principle is Square, a special type of Rectangle with equal adjacent sides. However, making a Square extending Rectangle violates the LSP principle.

Question 21

How do you call a subclass method if you are holding an object of the subclass in a reference variable of type superclass?

You can call a subclass method by first casting the object held by the reference variable of the superclass into the subclass. Once you hold the object in the subclass reference type, you can call methods from the subclass. See how type casting works in Java for more details.

That's all about **some frequently asked interview questions on Inheritance.** You should also know how `private` and `final` variables affect Inheritance. How can you extend a class with a private variable, and probably the difference between private and protected modifiers in Java? They are really important to understand and use Inheritance in Java. It's also worth noting that Inheritance is not the only way for code-resuse in Java, you can also use composition, whichis much more flexible. Joshua Bloch has advised in Effective Java that you should favor Compsoition over Inheritance and use Inheritance to define Type hierarchy rather than for code-reuse.

CHAPTER 4:
ADVANCED JAVA CLASSLOADER INTERVIEW QUESTIONS

Hello guys, if you are preparing for Java interviews and want to refresh your knowledge of Java Classloaders, you have baught the right book. I will share frequently asked Java interview questions about class loaders in this chapter. If you don't know, a class loader is a program that loads classes in Java programs. The class loading mechanism is crucial to understanding how the Java program works. When you run a Java program, you give the name of the main class, and from there onwards, built-in classloaders like Bootstrap classloader start loading not just the main classes but other Java library classes which is required to run that program.

JVM uses three main class loaders to load all the classes required to execute a Java program. They are Bootstrap class loader, Extension class loader, and System or Application class loader. Except for the BootStrap ClassLoader, all ClassLoader is implemented in Java and extends `java.lang.ClassLoader`, which is an abstract class in Java.

In this article, I have included basic and advanced class loader questions so that you can get decent ideas about how a class loader works in a core Java application and in a managed Java EE environment when web servers and application servers are involved.

15 Advanced Java ClassLoader Interview Questions and Answers

Here is my list of some of the frequently asked class loader-based questions from Java Interviews. This list is not complete but contains some interesting questions and highlights some essential concepts related to both class loading in Java and class loaders.

Question 1

What is ClassLoader in Java? From where do they load classes? And where is class-related metadata stored?

ClassLoader in Java is a class that is used to load other classes in Java virtual machines. This is the most frequently asked interview question about ClassLoader in Java. There are primarily three class loaders that are used by the JVM bootstrap class loader, extension class loader, and System or application class loader.

Except for the Bootstrap class loader, all ClassLoader is implemented in Java and extends `java.lang.ClassLoader`, which is an abstract class in Java. Also, all the class-related metadata, like a class definition, fields, and methods, are stored in the METASPACE part of JVM memory.

Every ClassLoader loads `.class` file from a particular location, BootStrap Classloader is responsible for loading System classes and loads the class file from rt.jar, extension class loader loads the class from `JRE/lib/ext` directory, and Application ClassLoader loads the class from the `CLASSPATH` environment variable, -classpath or -cp option while running Java application or from Class-path attribute of Manifest file of the JAR file in Java.

Question 2

How does ClassLoader work in Java?

This is another Java ClassLoader interview question that is getting popular, which is very good because a correct understanding of How ClassLoader works in Java is essential for any serious Java programmer.

ClassLoader works on the Delegation principle, where a request to load a class is delegated to the parent class loader before any attempt to load the class. If a parent doesn't find the class in its specified location, like CLASSPATH, the current Classloader searches for that class on its designated source and loads that Class.

Another important principle of class loading in Java is visibility. A class loaded by a parent is visible to All its child Classloaders but any class loaded by child ClassLoader is not visible to any parent ClassLoader, and an attempt to load a particular class that is only visible to Child will result in java.lang.NoClassDefFoundError in Java is one of the common Java errors related to class loading.

Question 3

What are the two rules of ClassLoader in Java?

As mentioned in the previous Java ClassLoader interview question, two rules of ClassLoader in Java are delegation and visibility. Delegation takes delegates' class loading requests to the parent class loader before trying. According to the visibility principle, all classes loaded by parent ClassLoader are visible to the child classloader.

Question 4

Can you implement your own ClassLoader in Java?

Yes, you can implement your own ClassLoader in Java, which can load .class files or any binary which can be translated or mapped into a .class file from any source like a database or network. You need to extend `java.lang.ClassLoader` is an abstract class that needs to override the `findClass()` method, which takes delegation.

Question 5

Can multiple classloaders in Java load the same class?

Yes, the Same class can be loaded by multiple ClassLoaders in Java. A class is uniquely identified by Java virtual machine by its fully qualified name and in the context of ClassLoader. This is a very useful feature of Java ClassLoader, which treats classes loaded from a different source even though they share a name, which is very much a possibility on Applets, where classes are normally downloaded from different sources.

Question 6

What does System.getClass().getClassLoader() return?

The `getClassLoader()` method of `java.lang.The  class` returns the class loader for the class, I mean, the name of ClassLoader which loaded that particular class.

The bootstrap class loader loads system classes like String or any other class from JDK, and they are implemented in the native language, mostly in C, and don't have the corresponding `java.lang.ClassLoader` instance. So, this call will return `null`.

```
System.out.println("System.getClass().getClassLoad
er() : " + System.class.getClassLoader());
Output : System.getClass().getClassLoader() : null
```

Question 7

Can you load a class that is not in CLASSPATH?

Yes, it's possible to load classes that are not in Classpath. Since Java Virtual Machine itself uses three different ClassLoader: BootStrap, extension, and System or Application class loaders, out of that, only Application ClassLoader uses CLASSPATH to search classes, and Extension ClassLoader loads a class from `jre/lib/ext` directory.

So if you put any Class in this directory, it will be loaded by Extension ClassLoader. You can even define your own ClassLoader, which can load classes from a network, database, or any other source. Though CLASSPATH is the most common place where Java searches for classes, it's not the only place.

Question 8

What is the extension ClassLoader in Java? From where does it load classes?

An extension class loader is one of three default class loaders that exist in the Java programming language. Extension class loader is a child of BootStrap ClassLoader and loads classes from the `jre/lib/ext` directory.

Sometimes programmers put class files in the `jre/lib/ext` directory, To avoid setting Java classpath, which works but it can create subtle issues like if you put a newer version of Class files on Classpath and expect your Java program to pick it from Classpath, either forgetting or not realizing that those classes already exist in `jre/lib/ext` directory.

Question 9

What is the binary name of a Class in Java?

What do you think? Can you answer this question? If you know, just answer in the comments, and I will put the first three people's names here who answered it correctly.

Question 10

What is the Context ClassLoader in Java?

Same here. Can you try to answer these questions without using Google? If you can, just answer, and I will put the first three people names here who answer this question correctly in the comments.

Question 11

Can two objects loaded from different ClassLoaders be equal in Java?

No, two objects loaded from different ClassLoaders cannot be the same. In the run time, a class is recognized by its fully qualified name and in the context of ClassLoader.

Multiple ClassLoaders can load the same class, common in Java EE environments with package hierarchies that distribute code in multiple JARs, such as WAR and EJB-JAR.

If you remember correctly, How to override the equals method in Java, you will see that the equals method has a check for `getClass()`, which will return false if two different ClassLoaders load it. If you don't have that check on `equals()` method, it will throw ClassCastException while comparing two classes loaded by different class loaders.

Question 12

Can Parent ClassLoader see classes loaded by Child ClassLoader in Java?

No, the Parent ClassLoader can not see classes loaded by the child ClassLoader in Java. As explained in a first ClassLoader interview question, Java Classloader works on the delegation principle, where a request to load a class is delegated to the parent ClassLoader.

But if the parent doesn't find the class and ultimately the child loads that class, it will not be visible to the parent ClassLoader, and any attempt to load that class from the parent ClassLoader will result in NoClassDefFoundError in Java.

Question 13

If you call `Class.forName()`, then which ClassLoader will load that particular class?

This is a very interesting ClassLoader interview question in Java. Class.forName() is an overloaded method in Java, and there are two versions of `Class.forName()` exists, where the overloaded version also accepts a ClassLoader instance which will be used to load and initialize the class.

A call to `Class.forName("binary name of Class)` is equivalent to Class.forName(className, true, currentLoader), which means the current ClassLoader will be used to load that class if it's not loaded already.

Question 14

Do the classloader loads all the classes at the start?

No, not all the classes are loaded by classloaders from the start. Only those which are needed are loaded. They follow lazy loading and only load the class when a static variable or method is invoked. You can also load a class using the `Class.forName()` method, which is often used to load JDBC driver classes from respective JAR Files.

That's all about **important questions related to class loaders in Java**. ClassLoader is a tricky concept to master, and not every Java developer pays attention to how Classworks as its rarely used in common Java development work but its always working, even if you run a simple Java program. At very minium, you should be familiar with different types of Classloader in Java and which classes are loaded by which class loaders, for example java.lang classes are loaded by which class loader? They play even more important role when you deploy Java application on web server and application server. You can use these interview questions to not only refresh your Classloader knowledge in Java but also prepare for Java interviews better.

CHAPTER 5:
JAVA ENUM INTERVIEW QUESTIONS

Enum was introduced in Java 5, and since then, it's been very popular among Java developers and widely used in different Java applications. Since Enum in Java is much more versatile than Enum in C or C++, it also presents many interesting use cases. But, despite being so popular, many Java programmers are still unaware of Enum's functionality and the subtle details of using Enum in Java code.

I realized this fact when a couple of my readers asked me questions like **Can Enum implement an interface in Java** or **Why we can not create Enum instances outside of Enum**, stating that these have been asked to them in their Java Interviews.

This motivates me to put together a list of frequently asked questions in Java Enum, which not only helps to do well in Interviews but also opens a new learning path.

As I had said before, a question in Interviews often makes you take a topic more seriously than otherwise, which is not bad. Given the power and facilities offered by Java Enum, I think it's high time to get a master of it.

Java Enum Interview Questions with Answers for 3 to 5 Years Experienced

Here is my list of questions based on the different features and properties of Java Enum. You can use this list for preparing an Interview or simply as a FAQ of Enum. If you are new to Java, I am sure you will learn a lot about Enum, which is a useful feature.

Question 1

Can Enum implement an interface in Java?

Yes, Enum can implement an interface in Java. Since an enum is a type similar to a `class` and interface, it can implement an interface. In some cases, this gives a lot of flexibility to use Enum as a specialized implementation.

Question 2

Can we use Enum in the switch case in Java?

Yes, you can use Enum in the Switch case in Java. That's one of the main advantages of using Enum. Since Enum instances are compile-time constants, you can safely use them inside `switch` and `case` statements.

Enum and Switch cases go well with each other, especially if Enum has a relatively small number of fixed constants like seven days in a week, 12 months in a year, etc.,

Question 3

How do you create Enum without any instance? Is it possible without compile-time error?

This is one of those tricky Java questions that the Interviewer loves to ask. Since Enum is viewed as a collection of a well-defined fixed number of instances like

Days of Week, and Months in a Year, having an Enum without any instance may seem awkward.

But yes, you can create Enum without any instance in Java, for creating a utility class. This is another innovative way of using Enum in Java.

Here is the code.

```java
public enum MessageUtil{
; // required to avoid compiler error, also
signifies no instance

public static boolean isValid() {
   throw new UnsupportedOperationException("Not
supported yet.");
}
}
```

Question 4

Can we override `toString()` method for Enum? What happens if we don't?

Of course, you can override toString in Enum, as like any other class, it also extends java.lang.Object and has toString() method available, but even if you don't override, you will not going to regret it much because the abstract base class of the enum does that for you and return the name, which is the name of the enum instance itself. here is the code of the toString() method from the Enum class :

```java
public String toString() {
   return name;
}
```

Name is set, when compiler emits code for creating enum in response to instance declaration in enum class itself, along with setting ordinal, as visible in this enum constructor from java.lang.Enum class :

```
protected Enum(String name, int ordinal) {
    this.name = name;
    this.ordinal = ordinal;
}
```

This is the only constructor for creating an enum, which is called by code, generated by the compiler in response to an enum type declaration in the Java program.

Question 5

Can we create an instance of Enum outside of Enum itself? If Not, Why?

No, you can not create enum instances outside of the Enum boundary because Enum doesn't have any public constructor, and the compiler doesn't allow you to provide any public constructor in Enum. Since the compiler generates much code in response to the enum type declaration, it doesn't allow public constructors inside Enum, which enforces declaring enum instances inside Enum itself.

Question 6

Can we declare Constructor inside Enum in Java?

This is asked along with the previous question on Java Enum. Yes, you can, but remember you can only declare either private or package-private constructor inside the enum. Public and protected constructors are not permitted inside the enum.

Question 7

What is the difference in comparing Enum with the == and equals() method?

Equals method of java.lang.Enum uses the == operator to check if two enums are equal. This means you can compare Enum using both the == and equals methods.

By the way, there are *subtle differences when you compare the enum with the ==* *and equals method,* which stems from == (equality operator) being an operator and equals() being a method.

1. Using == for comparing Enum can prevent NullPointerException

2. == method provides type safety during compile time

3. == should be faster than the equals method

Question 8

What does the ordinal() method do in Enum?

The ordinal method returns the order in which Enum instances are declared inside Enum. For example, in a DayOfWeek Enum, you can declare days in the order they come e.g.

```java
public enum DayOfWeek{
    MONDAY, TUESDAY, WEDNESDAY, THURSDAY, FRIDAY,
SATURDAY, SUNDAY;
}
```

Here if we call DayOfWeek.MONDAY.ordinal() will return 0, which is the first instance. This ordering can be very useful to represent real-world ordering, i.e., declaring TUESDAY after MONDAY ensures that it came after MONDAY and before WEDNESDAY.

Similarly, you can use an enum to represent the Month of the year in the order they come from, e.g., FEBRUARY after JANUARY and before MARCH.

All user-defined enum inherit this method from java.lang.Enum abstract class is set by the compiler when it internally calls the protected constructor of java.lang.Enum, which accepts name and ordinal.

Question 9

Can we use Enum with TreeSet or TreeMap in Java?

This is an interesting question on Java Enum. I would love to ask this to gauge knowledge of Enum until you know about `java.lang.Enum` and have looked at its code.

It's more likely that you don't know that **Enum implements a Comparable interface**, which is the main requirement to be used in Sorted Collections like TreeSet and TreeMap. Since Enum by default impalement `Comparable` interface, they can be safely used inside `TreeSet` or `TreeMap` in Java.

Question 10

What is the difference between the ordinal() and compareTo() in Enum?

This is a follow-up to the previous question on Java Enum. Actually, `compareTo()` mimics ordering provided by the `ordinal()` method, which is the natural order of Enum.

In short, Enum constraints are compared in the order they are declared. Also worth remembering is that enum constants are only comparable to other enum constants of the same enum type. Comparing the enum constant of one type to another type will result in a compiler error.

Question 11

Can Enum extend a class in Java?

No, Enum can not extend the class in Java. Surprised because I just said it's a type as a `class` or `interface` in Java. That is why this question is a good follow-up to the *previous Enum interview question.*

Since all Enum by default extends abstract base class `java.lang.Enum` they can not extend another class because Java doesn't support multiple inheritances for classes. Because of extending `java.lang.Enum` class, all enum gets methods like `ordinal()`, `values()`, or `valueOf()`.

Question 12

How to iterate over all instances of an Enum?

Well, if you have explored `java.lang.Enum`, you know that a values() method returns an array of all enum constants. Since every enum type implicitly extends `java.lang.Enum`, they get these `values()` method. Using this, you can iterate over all enum constants of a certain type.

Question 13

What are the advantages and disadvantages of using Enum as Singleton?

Enum provides you with a quick shortcut to implement the Singleton design pattern, and ever since it was mentioned in Effective Java, it's also been a popular choice.

On the face, Enum Singleton looks very promising and handles a lot of stuff for you, e.g., controlled instance creation, Serialization safety. On top of that, it's extremely easy to create thread-safe Singleton using Enum. You don't need to worry about double-checking locking and volatile variables anymore.

Question 14

What is the advantage of using Enum over an enum int pattern and an enum String pattern?

Suppose you have been coding for over five years and coded in JDK 1.3 and 1.4. In that case, you must be familiar with the Enum String pattern and enum int pattern, where we used *public static final constants* to represent a collection of a well-known fixed number of things like `DayOfWeek`.

There were a lot of problems with that approach like you don't have a dedicated enum type. Since it's a String variable representing days of the week, it can take any arbitrary value. Similarly, the *enum int pattern* can take any arbitrary value; the compiler doesn't prevent those.

By using Enum, you get this type-safety and compiler checking for you.

Question 15

How to convert a String to Enum in Java?

This is a day-to-day ask, given the popularity of String and Enum in Java application development. The best way for converting Enum to String is to declare a factory method inside Enum itself, which should take a String argument and return an Enum. You can choose to ignore the case as well.

That's all on this **list of Java 15 Enum Interview Questions and Answers**. Just remember though, reading is not enough for learning, it's just a first step. To get proficient with an enum, try to find out where you can use Enum in your project. This will give you REAL experience, and with real experience, you learn a lot more than a sample application because you tend to face more issues and handle the rather complex and detailed requirements. Nevertheless, these *Java 15 Enum questions* are still worth revising your knowledge, especially if you are rushing for an Interview and don't have enough time to explore Enum in detail.

CHAPTER 6:
JAVA ARRAYLIST INTERVIEW QUESTIONS

Hello guys, if you are preparing for Java interviews, then you have come to the right place. In this chapter, I will share some good Java interview questions based on the ArrayList class. I have hardly seen a Java interview without any questions from ArrayList, and why not? It's one of the most popular collection classes, and every Java developer uses it daily. Another reason for asking a question related to ArrayList is that you can ask a wide variety of questions to really check the breadth and depth of a candidate's knowledge.

To give you some idea about `ArrayList`, it's a collection class that implements the List interface. It's an alternative to an array data structure whose size you cannot change once created. ArrayList is a dynamic array that can grow and resize itself.

By implementing the List interface, it also got some properties like ordering, ArrayList keeps the element in the order they are inserted, and it also provides constant-time search operation if you know the index of an element like `get(index)` is O(1) operation.

This makes ArrayList an ideal choice when you are looking to retrieve values based on the index.

Contrary to search, adding and removing in ArrayList is a little costly because it can trigger re-sizing, which involves creating a new array and copying all elements from the old to a new one.

I am sure you know the basics, but you will learn more by reviewing some of these frequently asked Java ArrayList questions.

20+ ArrayList Questions with Answers from Java Interviews

So, let's start with the questions without wasting any more time. The questions are mainly divided into two categories. One is a fact-based question, which checks how much you know about ArrayList, and the other is a task-based question, which evaluates how good you are at doing things with ArrayList. In my list, I have combined both.

Question 1

How to remove duplicates from ArrayList in Java?

This is a task-based question. Since the List interface allows duplicates, ArrayList also allows it, but if you remember Set interface doesn't allow duplicates, which means you can remove duplicates from ArrayList by converting it into a Set and then back to ArrayList, but how will you keep the order intact? Well, you can use the LinkedHashSet, which keeps elements in the order they are inserted.

To remove duplicates from an ArrayList in Java using a LinkedHashSet, you can follow these steps:

1. Create an ArrayList with duplicate elements.

2. Create a new LinkedHashSet and add all elements of the ArrayList to it.

3. Create a new ArrayList and add all elements of the LinkedHashSet to it.

4. The new ArrayList will have all the elements of the original ArrayList with duplicates removed.

Here's an example:

```
ArrayList<Integer> listWithDuplicates = new
ArrayList<>(Arrays.asList(1, 2, 3, 2, 4, 3));
LinkedHashSet<Integer> set = new
LinkedHashSet<>(listWithDuplicates);
listWithDuplicates.clear();
listWithDuplicates.addAll(set);
```

In this example, the **ArrayList listWithDuplicates** is initialized with some duplicate elements. We create a **LinkedHashSet set** by passing the **listWithDuplicates** to its constructor. We then clear the **listWithDuplicates** and add all elements of the **set** back to the **listWithDuplicates**. The resulting **ArrayList** will only contain unique elements.

Question 2

How to reverse ArrayList in Java?

You can reverse ArrayList by using the `Collections.reverse()` method. There are a couple more ways, like iterating through the list and copying elements into a new one.

You can reverse an ArrayList in Java using the **Collections.reverse()** method. Here's an example:

```java
import java.util.ArrayList;
import java.util.Collections;

public class ReverseArrayListExample {
    public static void main(String[] args) {
        ArrayList<String> fruits = new ArrayList<>();
        fruits.add("apple");
        fruits.add("banana");
        fruits.add("cherry");
        fruits.add("date");

        System.out.println("Before reversing: " +
fruits);

        Collections.reverse(fruits);

        System.out.println("After reversing: " +
fruits);
    }
}
```

Output:

```
Before reversing: [apple, banana, cherry, date]
After reversing: [date, cherry, banana, apple]
```

In this example, we have an ArrayList of fruits and we're using the **Collections.reverse()** method to reverse the order of elements in the ArrayList. We're printing the ArrayList before and after reversing to demonstrate the effect.

Question 3

What is the difference between an array and an ArrayList in Java?

This is a fresher-level interview question. The main difference between an array and ArrayList is that the **former is static, and the latter is dynamic.** You cannot change the size of the array once created, but ArrayList can grow and increase its size automatically.

Question 4

How to synchronize ArrayList in Java?

This is a very good task-based question. If you remember, ArrayList is not thread-safe. It's not synchronized either, which means you cannot share it between multiple threads if one of them modifies it. Don't worry; you can synchronize ArrayList by using `Collections.synchronizedList()` method.

Question 5

When to use ArrayList and LinkedList in Java?

This is by far the most popular ArrayList based question from Java Interviews, and you can answer it very easily if you are familiar with two key data structures, array and linked list.

Since the array provides constant-time search operation, it's better to use ArrayList if search outnumbers add and remove operation. Otherwise, use LinkedList, which provides constant time add and remove operation.

Question 6

What is the difference between ArrayList and HashSet in Java?

One of the simplest questions you will ever see in a Java interview. The main difference is the former is List while the latter is Set which **means ArrayList allows duplicates** and keeps elements in order, while **HashSet doesn't allow duplicates** and provides no ordering guarantee.

Question 7

How to loop over ArrayList in Java?

There are many ways to traverse over ArrayList, you can use the classic for loop with index, or you can take an iterator from ArrayList and can use a while loop in conjunction with Iterator.hasNext() method, Or you can use the new for each loop introduced in Java 5, which doesn't require an index.

Question 8

What is the difference between Vector and ArrayList in Java?

This is the second most popular question based on ArrayList in Java. Though both Vector and ArrayList implement List interface, Vector is synchronized while ArrayList is not synchronized, which means the former is thread-safe and fast while the latter is not thread-safe and slow.

Question 9

How to create and initialize ArrayList in one line?

There is a nice little trick to do this by using the `Arrays.asList()` method, but remember the List returned by this class has some differences with ArrayList. From Java 9 onwards you can also use List.of() method to create and initialize List in same line

```
ArrayList<String> fruits = new
ArrayList<>(Arrays.asList("apple", "banana", "orange"));
```

In this example, we create an ArrayList of Strings named **fruits** and initialize it with three elements: "apple", "banana", and "orange". The **Arrays.asList()** method converts the array of elements into a List, which is then used to initialize the ArrayList. The constructor of ArrayList that takes a Collection as argument is used to create the ArrayList.

Question 10

How to sort ArrayList in Java?

Another task-based ArrayList interview question. You can easily sort the ArrayList by using the `Collections.sort()` method. All you need to do is make sure that elements implement either the Comparable or Comparator interface. The former is used to sort in the natural order which is increasing order for a List with numbers, while the latter is used while sorting in the custom order.

Here's an example:

```java
import java.util.ArrayList;
import java.util.Collections;

public class SortArrayListExample {
    public static void main(String[] args) {
        ArrayList<Integer> numbers = new
ArrayList<Integer>();
        numbers.add(3);
        numbers.add(1);
        numbers.add(4);
        numbers.add(2);

        System.out.println("Before sorting: " +
numbers);

        Collections.sort(numbers);

        System.out.println("After sorting: " + numbers);
    }
}
```

Output:

Before sorting: [3, 1, 4, 2]

After sorting: [1, 2, 3, 4]

In the example above, we first create an **ArrayList** of integers and add some elements to it. Then, we print the elements of the **ArrayList** before sorting. Next, we call the **Collections.sort()** method to sort the elements in ascending order. Finally, we print the elements of the **ArrayList** after sorting.

Question 11

What is the difference between HashMap and ArrayList in Java?

There is a huge difference between HashMap and ArrayList. Fundamental is the former is a Map data structure that stores key-value pairs while the latter stores just an object. HashMap access objects using a key, while ArrayList accesses elements using an index. Though both provide `O(1)` search performance, ArrayList's performance is guaranteed, but HashMap can vary depending upon the collision level.

Question 12

How to use ArrayList in Java?

You can use ArrayList in Java for storing objects where you want fast search with index as well you want to keep them in the order they are inserted into the list. ArrayList also allows duplicates.

Question 13

How to convert ArrayList to String in Java?

Simple, just call `toString()`, right? Unfortunately, the String representation is not very helpful. If you are looking for a comma-separated String containing all elements of ArrayList, then you can either use StringBuilder or Java 8 String joiner or some older library method.

Here's an example using **StringBuilder**:

```java
import java.util.ArrayList;

public class ArrayListToStringExample {
    public static void main(String[] args) {
        ArrayList<String> list = new ArrayList<>();
        list.add("apple");
        list.add("banana");
        list.add("cherry");

        StringBuilder sb = new StringBuilder();
        for (String s : list) {
            sb.append(s);
            sb.append(", ");
        }
        sb.delete(sb.length() - 2, sb.length()); // remove last comma and space

        String result = sb.toString();
        System.out.println(result);
    }
}
```

Alternatively, you can use the **String.join()** method, like this:

```java
String result = String.join(", ", list);
```

This will print output:

apple, banana, cherry

Question 14

How to get a sublist from ArrayList in Java?

This is another task-based question, but you can easily do it if you remember API. You can get a list of elements in a range by using the `subList()` method from the ArrayList class. This would be very helpful in case of a sorted list.

This method takes two parameters, the starting index and the ending index (exclusive) of the sublist. Here's an example:

```
ArrayList<Integer> numbers = new ArrayList<Integer>();
numbers.add(1);
numbers.add(2);
numbers.add(3);
numbers.add(4);
numbers.add(5);

List<Integer> sublist = numbers.subList(1, 4);

System.out.println(sublist); // [2, 3, 4]
```

In this example, we created an ArrayList of integers, added some elements to it, and then used the **subList()** method to get a sublist of elements from index 1 (inclusive) to index 4 (exclusive). The resulting sublist contains the elements [2, 3, 4].

Question 15

What is the difference between the length() of the array and the size() of ArrayList in Java?

This is one of the tricky questions. If you get the backed array and call the length(), it will return how many elements you can store in this array, also known as capacity, but if you call the size() function of the ArrayList class, then it will return a total number of elements currently stored in ArrayList, which is always less than or equal to capacity.

Question 16

What is CopyOnWriteArrayList in Java?

It's a concurrent collection class that is introduced as an **alternative to synchronized Lists in Java**. This class takes advantage of the advanced thread-safety technique instead of locking. It's very efficient if ArrayList is mostly used for reading purposes because it allows multiple threads to read data without locking, which was not possible with synchronized ArrayList.

Question 17

How to remove objects from ArrayList in Java?

There are two ways to remove elements from ArrayList. First, you can call the `remove(int  index)` method and pass on the index of the element you want to remove, and second, you can call the `remove(Object  obj)` method and pass the element you want to remove. By the way, just be careful while working with an ArrayList of integers because autoboxing can cause issues by creating an ambiguity between two remove methods.

Here is an example of removing objects form ArrayList using Iterator and matching condition:

```
ArrayList<Integer> list = new ArrayList<>();
list.add(1);
list.add(2);
list.add(3);
list.add(4);
list.add(5);

Iterator<Integer> iterator = list.iterator();
while (iterator.hasNext()) {
    if (iterator.next() % 2 == 0) {
        iterator.remove(); // remove even numbers
    }
}
```

Question 18

How to make ArrayList read-only in Java?

Another task and API-based interview question. You can answer it easily if you are about the Collections utility class, which provides several wrappers of the standard ArrayList class, e.g., you can use Collections to create a synchronized version or read-only version of ArrayList in Java. From Java 11 onwards, you can make an **ArrayList** read-only by wrapping it in an unmodifiable list using the **Collections.unmodifiableList()** method. This creates an unmodifiable view of the original list, so any attempts to modify the list will result in an **UnsupportedOperationException**.

Here's an example of how to make an **ArrayList** read-only:

```java
List<String> originalList = new ArrayList<>();
originalList.add("one");
originalList.add("two");
originalList.add("three");

List<String> readOnlyList =
Collections.unmodifiableList(originalList);

// Attempting to modify the read-only list will throw an
UnsupportedOperationException
readOnlyList.add("four"); // Throws
UnsupportedOperationException
```

In this example, we create an **ArrayList** called **originalList** with three elements. We then create a read-only view of **originalList** by wrapping it in an unmodifiable list using **Collections.unmodifiableList()**. Finally, we attempt to add a new element to the read-only list, which results in an **UnsupportedOperationException**.

It's important to note that although the read-only list cannot be modified directly, it is still possible to modify the original list. Any changes made to the original list will be reflected in the read-only view. If you need to ensure that the list cannot be modified in any way, you should consider making a defensive copy of the list before wrapping it in an unmodifiable view. **Question 19**

How to sort ArrayList in descending order in Java?

This is the follow-up question to one of the previous questions related to sorting. By default, elements are sorted in increasing order as this is how their `compareTo()` or compare() method compares them. If you want to sort into descending order, just reverse the comparison logic using the `Collections` `.reverseComparator()` or Collections.revrseOrder() method.

Here's an example of how to sort an **ArrayList** in descending order:

```
List<Integer> list = new ArrayList<>();
list.add(5);
list.add(2);
list.add(8);
list.add(1);

// Sort the list in descending order
Collections.sort(list, Collections.reverseOrder());

// Print the sorted list
System.out.println(list); // Output: [8, 5, 2, 1]
```

In this example, we create an **ArrayList** called **list** with four elements. We then sort the list in descending order using the **Collections.sort()** method and passing **Collections.reverseOrder()** as the **Comparator**. This method returns a **Comparator** that sorts the elements in reverse order. Finally, we print the sorted list to the console.

You can use this same approach to sort an **ArrayList** of any type in descending order, as long as you provide an appropriate **Comparator** for that type.

That's all about **ArrayList questions from Java Interviews**. I have covered almost everything I know, which has been asked previously of many Java programmers, both freshers and experienced with 2 to 5 years of experience. Some companies which give more importance to coding skills can also ask you to implement your own ArrayList class in Java, so be prepared for that also. You can always use an array to implement ArrayList in Java.

CHAPTER 7:
JAVA HASHMAP INTERVIEW QUESTIONS

The `java.util.HashMap` is one of the workhorses of JDK. Along with ArrayList, it is one of the most used classes from Java's collection framework. There is hardly a real-world Java project where I haven't seen the use of `HashMap`. It is an implementation of a hash table data structure, and it's not a surprise that `HashMap` is so useful. As someone has rightly said, *"if you could have just one data structure, make it a hash table."* The hash table data structure allows you to search for a value in O(1) time if you have a key. In Java, several implementations of hash table data structures exist, like `Hashtable`, `ConcurrentHashMap`, `LinkedHashMap`, etc., but `HashMap` is your general-purpose map.

Though, if you have a special need, you can use other hash table implementations available in JDK. For example, if you want to preserve the order of mapping, then you can consider using `LinkedHashMap`. If you wish to keep mappings sorted, then you can use `TreeMap`, which is a sorted map implementation.

Similarly, if you need a hash table implementation that is thread-safe and can be used in a concurrent application without compromising the Scalability, then consider using a `ConcurrentHashMap` from JDK 5.

Java HashMap Interview Questions

Here is my list of HashMap questions from Java Interviews. This list includes questions based on the internal implementation of HashMap, the Map API, how you use HashMap, and standard best practices while using HashMap in a Java application.

Question 1

How does the put() method of HashMap works in Java?

The put() method of HashMap works in the principle of hashing. It is responsible for storing an object in the backend array. The hashcode() method is used in conjunction with a hash function to find the correct location for the object in the bucket. If a collision occurs, then the entry object, which contains both key and value, is added to a linked list, and that linked list is stored in the bucket location.

Question 2

What is the requirement for an object to be used as a key or value in HashMap?

The key or value object must implement the equals() and hashcode() methods. The hash code is used when you insert the key object into the map, while equals are used when you try to retrieve a value from the map.

Question 3

What will happen if you try to store a key that is already present in HashMap?

If you store an existing key in the HashMap, then it will override the old value with the new value, and put() will return the old value. There will not be any exceptions or errors.

Question 4

Can you store a null key in Java HashMap?

Yes, HashMap allows one null key, which is stored at the first location of the bucket array, e.g., `bucket[0]` = `value`. The HashMap doesn't call hashCode() on the null key because it will throw NullPointerException. Hence when a user calls the `get()` method with null, then the value of the first index is returned.

Question 5

Can you store a null value inside HashMap in Java?

Yes, HashMap also allows null values; you can store as many null values as you want, as shown in the hashmap example post in this blog.

Question 6

How does HashMap handle collisions in Java?

The java.util.HashMap uses chaining to handle collisions, which means new entries, an object which contains both key and values, are stored in a linked list along with the existing value, and then that linked list is stored in the bucket location.

In the worst case, where all key has the same hashcode, your hash table will be turned into a linked list, and searching for a value will take `O(n)` time as opposed to `O(1)` time.

If you want to learn more about hash table data structure, I suggest you consult a good data structure and algorithm course like these best data structures and algorithms courses, which cover not only basic data structures like an array, linked list, binary tree, and hash table but also advanced concepts like O(n) sorting algorithms, Radix sort, Counting sort, etc.

Question 7

Which data structure does HashMap represent?

The `HashMap` is an implementation of a hash table data structure, which is idle for mapping one value to another, like ID to name, as you can search for value in O(1) time if you have the key.

Question 8

Which data structure is used to implement HashMap in Java?

Even though `HashMap` represents a hash table, it is internally implemented by using an array and linked list data structure in JDK. The array data structure is used as a bucket, while a linked list is used to store all mappings which land in the same bucket. From Java 8 onwards, the linked list is dynamically replaced by a binary search tree once a number of elements in the linked list cross a certain threshold to improve performance.

Question 9

Can you store a duplicate key in HashMap?

No, you cannot insert duplicate keys in HashMap. It doesn't allow duplicate keys. If you try to insert an existing key with the new or same value, then it will override the old value, but the size of HashMap will not change, i.e., it will remain the same. This is one of the reasons why you get all keys from the HashMap by calling keySet(). It returns a Set, not a Collection because a Set doesn't allow duplicates.

Question 10

Can you store the duplicate value in Java HashMap?

Yes, you can put duplicate values in the HashMap of Java. It allows duplicate values; that's why when you retrieve all values from the Hashmap by calling the values() method, it returns a Collection and not a Set. Worth noting is that it doesn't return List because HashMap doesn't provide any ordering guarantee for key or value.

Question 11

Is HashMap thread-safe in Java?

No, HashMap is not a thread-safe in Java. You should not share a HashMap with multiple threads if one or more thread is modifying the HashMap, e.g., inserting or removing a map. Though, you can easily share a read-only `HashMap`.

Question 12

What will happen if you use HashMap in a multithreaded Java application?

If you use HashMap in a multithreaded environment in such a way that multiple threads structurally modify the map like add, remove or modify mapping, then the internal data structure of HashMap may get corrupt like some links may go missing, some may point to incorrect entries, and the map itself may become completely useless. Hence, it is advised not to use HashMap in the concurrent application; instead, you should use a thread-safe map, e.g., `ConcurrentHashMap` or Hashtable.

Question 13

What are the different ways to iterate over HashMap in Java?

Here are some of the ways to iterate over HashMap in Java:

- ➢ by using keySet and iterator
- ➢ by using entrySet and iterator
- ➢ by using entrySet and enhanced for loop
- ➢ by using the keySet and get() method

Question 14

How do you remove a mapping while iterating over HashMap in Java?

Even though HashMap provides a `remove()` method to remove a key and a key/value pair, you cannot use them to remove a mapping while traversing a HashMap. Instead, you need to use the Iterator's remove method to remove a mapping, as shown in the following example:

```
Iterator itr = map.entrySet().iterator();

while(itr.hasNext()){
  Map.Entry current = itr.next();

  if(current.getKey().equals("matching"){
    itr.remove(); // this will remove the current
  entry.
  }
}
```

You can see that we have used `Iterator.remove()` method to remove the current entry while traversing the map.

Question 15

In which order are mappings stored in HashMap?

Random order because HashMap doesn't provide any ordering guarantee for keys, values, or entries. When you iterate over a HashMap, you may get a different order every time you iterate over it.

Question 16

Can you sort HashMap in Java?

No, you cannot sort a HashMap because, unlike List, it is not an ordered collection. Albeit, you can sort the contents of HashMap by keys, values, or by entries by sorting and then storing the result into an ordered map like LinkedHashMap or a sorted map, e.g., TreeMap.

Question 17

What is the load factor in HashMap?

A **load factor** is a number that controls the resizing of HashMap when a number of elements in the HashMap cross the load factor as if the load factor is 0.75 and when becoming more than 75% full, then resizing trigger which involves array copy.

Question 18

How does resize happen in HashMap?

The resizing happens when the map becomes full or when the size of the map crosses the load factor. For example, if the load factor is 0.75 and then becomes more than 75% full, then resizing trigger, which involves an array copy. First, the size of the bucket is doubled, and then old entries are copied into a new bucket.

Question 19

How many entries can you store in HashMap? What is the maximum limit?

There is no maximum limit for HashMap. You can store as many entries as you want because when you run out of the bucket, entries will be added to a linked list that can support an infinite number of entries, of course, until you exhaust all the memory you have.

Btw, the `size()` method of HashMap returns an `int`, which has a limit. Once a number of entries cross the limit, `size()` will overflow, and if your program relies on that, then it will break.

This issue has been addressed in JDK 8 by introducing a new method called `mappingCount()`, which returns a long value. So, you should use `mappingCount()` for large maps.

Question 20

What is the difference between the capacity and size of HashMap in Java?

The `capacity` denotes how many entries HashMap can store, and size denotes how many mappings or key/value pair is currently present.

Question 21

What will happen if two different keys of HashMap return the same hashcode()?

If two keys of HashMap return the same hash code, then they will end up in the same bucket; hence collision will occur. They will be stored in a linked list together.

That's all about **important Java HashMap interview questions**. I have tried to answer them as well, but if you disagree with an answer, then feel free to comment. Since `HashMap` is a very important class in Java and equally important from the Java interview point of view, it pays to understand this class and its implementation in depth. These questions will not only help you to understand HashMap better but also encourage you to find out more about `HashMap`, its Java implementation, and hash table data structure in general.

CHAPTER 8:
JAVA CONCURRENTHASHMAP INTERVIEW QUESTIONS

The `ConcurrentHashMap` class part of the concurrent collections package added on JDK 1.5, which contains utility classes like `BlockingQueue`, `CopyOnWriteArrayList`, `CopyOnWriteArraySet`, etc. It is a replacement of synchronized hash-based map implementations, e.g., Hashtable and synchronized `HashMap`. It implements `Map` and `ConcurrentMap` (a sub-interface of Map) interface, which allows you to store key-value pairs. The class is similar to HashMap or Hashtable, but it's more **scalable** and the right fit for concurrent Java applications. Unlike `Hashtable`, which achieves its thread safety by compromising the scalability, `ConcurrentHashMap` uses advanced techniques, e.g., dividing the map into segments to remain thread-safe and scalable at the same time.

Because of its performance and scalability, as well as thread safety, it is the most popular choice of Map in concurrent Java applications.

In general, replacing synchronized collections with a concurrent collection can dramatically improve the scalability of your Java application with little risk.

Anyway, let's start with this list of Java interview questions based on `ConcurrentHashMap` class and the concepts around it.

10 Java ConcurrentHashMap Interview Questions with Answers

Here are some of the best and frequently asked Java `ConcurrentHashMap` interview questions. These questions are collected from the real interview. Hence, don't be surprised if you have already seen them during interviews.

These questions will not only help you to do well in interviews but also encourage you to learn more about the concurrent hash map, which will eventually help you in your day-to-day programming job.

Question 1

What is **ConcurrentHashMap** in Java?

The `java.util.concurrent.ConcurrentHashMap` is a concurrent collection class added on JDK 1.5 as a replacement for synchronized hash-based map implementations, e.g., Hashtable and synchronized HashMap. They offer better performance and scalability over their synchronized counterparts with little risk.

Question 2

Does **ConcurrentHashMap** thread-safe in Java?

Yes, `ConcurrentHashMap` is thread-safe in Java, which means two threads can modify the map without damaging its internal data structure, e.g., array and linked list. If you compare this to `HashMap`, which is not thread-safe, exposing HashMap to multiple threads **may damage internal data structure** and may render the map completely useless, where many links may go missing or point to the wrong elements.

Question 3

How does `ConcurrentHashMap` achieve thread safety?

The `java.util.ConcurrentHashMap` achieves thread safety by dividing the map into segments and locking only the segment, which requires instead of locking the whole map. So, yes, it achieves thread safety using locking, but it performs better because, unlike HashMap, **it never locks the whole map**. This technique is also known as lock stripping.

Question 4

Can multiple threads read from `ConcurrentHashMap` same time?

Yes, `ConcurrentHashMap` allows concurrent reading without locking, as reading operation doesn't require locking or thread safety.

Question 5

Can one thread read and the other write on `ConcurrentHashMap` at the same time?

Yes, it's possible for a small number of writes. For example, if a write operation is modifying one segment of `ConcurrentHashmap` and a read operation is happening on other segments, then a reader will not block, but if the reader thread is also trying to read from the same segment, then it will block until the writer is done.

Question 6

How does `ConcurrentHashMap` work internally?

The `java.util.ConcurrentHashMap` works similarly to `HashMap` when it comes to storing key/value pairs and retrieving values. The only difference in its implementation comes from the concurrency perspective and how it achieves thread safety. It divides the map into several segments, by default 16, also known as synchronization level.

Because of this, concurrent `get()`, `put()`, `contains()` operation is possible because it never locks the whole map, but only the relevant segment is locked. This means readers can access the map concurrency with writers, and a limited number of writers can modify the map concurrently. The result is better throughput and Scalability.

Here is a diagram that explains how a segment looks like in a `ConcurrentHashMap` of Java. Basically, it's nothing but a mini hash table with a bucket and a linked list of hash entries in case of collision:

Since the Iterator returned by `ConcurrentHashMap` is weakly consistent, the recent concurrency modification may or may not be visible to it. There is no guarantee offered on such an operation.

Question 7

How do you atomically update a value in `ConcurrentHashMap`?

If you want to atomically update an existing value in `ConcurrentHashMap`, you can use the `replace()` function of concurrent hashmap.

It accepts both old values and new values and only updates the map if the existing value in the map matches with the old value provided. This means the map is not concurrently modified during its call.

If the existing value is changed and does not match with the old value, then replace fails and returns false. You can use call the `replace()` method in the while loop until you succeed, as shown below:

```
ConcurrentMap<String, Long> populationByCities =
new ConcurrentHashMap<>();
do{
  Long currentValue = populationByCities.get("New
York");
```

```
    Long newValue = currentValue == null ? 1 :
currentValue + 1;
}while(!populationByCities.replace("New York",
currentValue, newValue));
```

Question 8

How do you remove a mapping while iterating over **ConcurrentHashMap?**

You can use an Iterator to remove the mapping from ConcurrentHashMap in Java, as shown below:

```
Map<String, Integer> bookAndPrice = new
ConcurrentHashMap<>();
bookAndPrice.put("Effective Java", 42);
bookAndPrice.put("Head First Java", 29);
bookAndPrice.put("Java Concurrency in Practice", 33);
bookAndPrice.put("Head First Design Patterns",
41);

System.out.println("before removing : " +
bookAndPrice);
Iterator<String> iterator =
bookAndPrice.keySet().iterator();

while(iterator.hasNext()){
  if(iterator.next().contains("Java")){
   iterator.remove();
  }
}
System.out.println("after removing : " +
bookAndPrice);

Output
before removing : {Java Concurrency in
Practice=33,
```

```
Head First Design Patterns=41, Effective Java=42,
Head First Java=29}
after removing : {Head First Design Patterns=41}
```

Question 9

Does the Iterator of `ConcurrentHashMap` fail-safe or fail-fast?

The Iterator of `ConcurrentHashMap` is a fail-safe iterator which means it will not throw a ConcurrentModificationException, thus, eliminating the need to lock the map during iteration.

The Iterator returned by `ConcurrentHashMap` is also weakly consistent, which means if the Map is modified during iteration, it may or may not reflect the recent modification. Generally, it creates a copy of the collection before iterating.

Question 10

What will happen if you add a new mapping in `ConcurrentHashMap` while one thread is iterating over it?

This is one of the tricky questions related to `ConcurrentHashMap`. Since iterators of `ConcurrentHashMap` are weakly consistent and fail-safe, they will not fail with `ConcurrentModificationException,` but it's also possible that they won't see any modification once iteration starts. Even though it's implementation-dependent, JDK generally creates a separate copy of ConcurrentHashMap for iteration instead of iterating over an original copy.

Question 11

Can you pass an object of ConcurrentHahsMap when a Map is expected?

Yes, because `ConcurrentHashMap` implements `java.util.concur rent.ConcurrentMap` interface, which extends `java.util.Map` interface, hence `ConcurrentHashMap` IS-A Map. Also, you can store an object of `ConcurrentHashMap` into a Map variable as shown below:

```
Map<String, Integer> bookAndPrice = new
ConcurrentHashMap<>();
```

Though, this means you may not have access to methods declared in the java.util.concurrent.`ConcurrentHashMap` class, e.g., `forEachKey()` or `forEachValue()` method added in Java 8.

That's all about some of the **frequently asked questions about ConcurrentHashMap in Java interviews**. These questions will not only help you to do well in your job interview but also encourage you to learn more about `ConcurrentHashMap`. Solid knowledge of `ConcurrentHashMap` is expected from both junior and senior Java developers, given its importance and usability in every Java application. At least you should be comfortable with day-to-day operations with `ConcurrentHashMap` and understand how the internal implementation works, especially when compared to other thread-safe map implementations like Hashtable and Synchronized HashMap.

CHAPTER 9:
JAVA DATE, TIME, AND CALENDAR INTERVIEW QUESTIONS

The Date and Time API is a significant one for day-to-day Java development work, but many interviewers don't ask enough questions on this topic. Most of the questions are based on either Java Collection framework like `HashMap`, `ConcurrentHashMap`, or `ArrayList` or multi-threading concepts like `volatile`, `synchronized,` and atomic variables. This is not good, and many interviewers have realized that a good understanding of date and time API is also important for a good Java developer. That's the main reason for the increasing date, time, and calendar-based Java interview questions in recent times, particularly in the last couple of years.

Since the Java development job market is perfect at this moment. There are many jobs open, particularly in the investment banking domain in Asia Pacific. It's probably the best time to change your job, especially if you are stuck with no learning, no salary increment, and not a significant bonus or incentive in the last couple of years.

Apart from stability, growth is significant because if you don't move forward, you will be stuck and eventually move backward; hence, changing jobs is as important as sticking to a working job.

Top 22 Date, Time, and Calendar Interview Questions and Answers

I have been sharing interview questions on various Java topics for the last couple of years, like multithreading, collections, design patterns, coding problems, etc. Still, one topic I haven't touched on yet is date and time, and that's why I thought to share some of the interesting Date and time-based questions from recent Java interviews. In this article, you will find those.

Question 1

Does SimpleDateFormat be safe to use in the multithreaded program?

Unfortunately, DateFormat and all its implementations, including `SimpleDateFormat,` are not thread-safe; hence, it should not be used in the multi-threaded program until external thread-safety measures are applied, e.g., confining `SimpleDateFormat` object into a ThreadLocal variable. If you don't do that, you will get an incorrect result while parsing or formatting dates in Java. Though, for all practical date-time purposes, I highly recommend the joda-time library.

Question 2

How do you format a date in Java? Like in the ddMMyyyy format?

You can either use the `SimpleDateFormat` class or the joda-time library to format the date in Java. DateFormat class allows you to format data in many popular formats. From Java 8 onwards you can also use new Date and Time API and DateFormatter class to format a date in Java.

Here's an example of how to format a date in the **ddMMyyyy** format using Java 8:

```
import java.time.LocalDate;
import java.time.format.DateTimeFormatter;

public class DateExample {
    public static void main(String[] args) {
        LocalDate date = LocalDate.now();
        DateTimeFormatter formatter =
DateTimeFormatter.ofPattern("ddMMyyyy");
        String formattedDate = date.format(formatter);
        System.out.println("Formatted date: " +
formattedDate);
    }
}
```

In this example, we first get the current date using the **LocalDate.now()** method. Then, we create a **DateTimeFormatter** object using the **ofPattern()** method, passing in the desired date format as a string. Finally, we format the date using the **format()** method of the **LocalDate** class and print the result to the console.

Question 3

Can you tell some differences between the old and new Date Time API of Java 8?

Even though the new Date and Time APIs are completely new APIs, you can deduce the following difference between them:

1) In the old API, Date was mutable, but in Java 8, all date and time classes like LocalDate, LocalTime, or LocalDateTime are Immutable.

2) In the old API, SimpleDateFormat was not thread-safe, but in Java 8, Formatter is thread-safe.

3) In the old Date and Calendar API, the Year starts with 1900, and Months start with 0, which is corrected in Java 8; here, the numbers make more sense.

4) Old Date and Calendar API has just one class, Date, to represent date and time, but Java 8 has separated classes for Date and Time, e.g., LocalDate and LocalTime

Question 4

Which date does the following Date instance represent?

```
Date aDate = new Date(2015, 12, 25, 20, 40);
```

This is a tricky question for casual Java developers who have no written date and time-based code because this will not represent Christmas day or 25th December 2015. This code has got two bugs. First, the year starts in 1900 and represents 2015. You need to pass 115, i.e., 2015-1900.

The second issue with this code is that the month is not correct. The month starts from 0, so December would be 11, not 12. Interesting right? That's why you should use the new Date and Time API from Java 8, which solves all these issues.

Question 5

How do you copy a Date in Java?

It's a simple question to answer. The Date class implements the clone() method, so just call the `date.clone()` to create a copy of the Date object in Java.

Question 6

What is the relationship between java.sql.Date and java.util.Date?

This is one of the exciting questions as not many developers know this fine but obvious detail. The `java.sql.Date` extends java.util.Date and suppresses all time-related methods to act as just a date class. This is in direct violation of the Liskov substitution principle.

Question 7

Can you format Calendar in Java?

No, the Calendar cannot be formatted in Java. You can only format dates.

Question 8

How do you convert a Calendar to a Date and vice versa?

Well, you can use the `Calendar.setTime()` and `Calendar.getTime()` methods to convert the Calendar to Date and vice-versa.

Question 9

What is the equivalent of a Date class in Java 8?

Instance class is the equivalent to `java.util.Date` in Java 8 because it also represents a millisecond value or an instance in the timescale. Java 8 has also added conversion methods, e.g., `toInstant()` and `fromDate()`, to convert the instance to `java.util.Date` and vice-versa.

Question 10

How do you convert a millisecond to a Date in Java?

One of the simplest questions to answer is the `getTime()` method, which returns the millisecond from the Epoch.

Question 11

How do you get a month and year from a Date object in Java?

You can convert a Date to a Calendar and then use its `get()` method with various fields to get the month, year, day of the week, and other date particulars e.g.

```
int day = calendar.get(Calendar.DATE); // returns the day
int month = calendar.get(Calendar.MONTH) + 1; // month
starts from 0
int year = calendar.get(Calendar.YEAR) + 1900; // year
starts from 1900
```

Better, you should use Java 8 API . In Java 8, you can use the **java.time** package to get a month and year from a **java.util.Date** object. Here's an example:

```
import java.time.LocalDate;
import java.time.YearMonth;
import java.time.ZoneId;
import java.util.Date;

public class DateExample {
   public static void main(String[] args) {
     Date date = new Date();
     LocalDate localDate =
date.toInstant().atZone(ZoneId.systemDefault()).toLocalD
ate();

     // Get the month and year from the date
     int month = localDate.getMonthValue();
     int year = localDate.getYear();

     // Alternatively, you can use YearMonth to get the
month and year
     YearMonth yearMonth = YearMonth.from(localDate);

     System.out.println("Month: " + month);
     System.out.println("Year: " + year);
     System.out.println("YearMonth: " + yearMonth);
   }
}
```

In this example, we first convert the **Date** object to a **LocalDate** object using the **toInstant()** method and the system default time zone. Then we can use the **getMonthValue()** and **getYear()** methods to get the month and year from the **LocalDate** object. Alternatively, we can use the **YearMonth** class to get the year and month together.

Question 12

How do you convert XMLGregorianCalendar to Date in Java?

To convert an **XMLGregorianCalendar** object to a **Date** object in Java, you can use the **toGregorianCalendar()** method to convert **XMLGregorianCalendar** to **GregorianCalendar** and then use the **getTime()** method of **GregorianCalendar** to get a **Date** object. Here's an example:

```java
import javax.xml.datatype.XMLGregorianCalendar;
import java.util.Calendar;
import java.util.Date;
import java.util.GregorianCalendar;

public class XmlGregorianCalendarToDateExample {
    public static void main(String[] args) {
        // Create an XMLGregorianCalendar object with the
current date and time
        XMLGregorianCalendar xmlGregorianCalendar =
javax.xml.datatype.DatatypeFactory.newInstance().newXMLGr
egorianCalendar(new GregorianCalendar());

        // Convert XMLGregorianCalendar to Date
        Date date =
xmlGregorianCalendar.toGregorianCalendar().getTime();

        // Print the Date object
        System.out.println(date);
    }
}
```

In the above example, we first create an **XMLGregorianCalendar** object with the current date and time using **javax.xml.datatype.DatatypeFactory .newInstance().newXMLGregorianCalendar(new GregorianCalendar())**.

Then, we use the **toGregorianCalendar()** method to convert **XMLGregorianCalendar** to **GregorianCalendar**, and then call the **getTime()** method of **GregorianCalendar** to get a **Date** object.

Finally, we print the **Date** object using **System.out.println**

Question 13

How do you get the current time in GMT in Java?

The Java date is independent of time and displays time in a current time zone only if you print them. So, to convert the current time to GMT, you need to use a Calendar with a time zone as shown in the given answer. Alternatively, you can also use Java 8 Date and Time API. For example, To get the current time in GMT (Greenwich Mean Time) in Java, you can use the **java.time.OffsetDateTime** class along with the **java.time.ZoneOffset** class. Here's an example code snippet:

```
OffsetDateTime now = OffsetDateTime.now(ZoneOffset.UTC);
System.out.println("Current time in GMT: " + now);
```

In the above code, **OffsetDateTime.now()** creates an instance of **OffsetDateTime** with the current date and time, and **ZoneOffset.UTC** sets the time zone to GMT. The resulting **OffsetDateTime** object represents the current time in GMT.

Question 14

Is the java.util.Date class Immutable in Java?

No, the **Date is not immutable**. You can change its internal to represent a different date. This is why when you have **a member variable which represent Date**, you must be careful not to leak its reference outside using the `getDate()` method because then the client can modify the state of the Immutable object. Instead, a copy should be returned to the client. Alternatively, you should use LocalDate, LocalTime, and LocalDateTime classes from Java 8 API which are both immutable and preffered in new code.

Question 15

How do you add and subtract a day, month, and year in a Date object?

This is one of the common day-to-day tasks of a Java developer. In Java, you can add and subtract a day, month, and year from a **Date** object using the **Calendar** class or you can use Java 8 Date and Time classes like **LocalDate**, **LocalTime**, and **LocalDateTime** to get the current date and time, create a specific date, and manipulate dates by adding and subtracting days and months.

Here is an example:

```java
import java.time.LocalDate;
import java.time.LocalTime;
import java.time.LocalDateTime;
import java.time.Month;

public class DateTimeExample {
    public static void main(String args[]) {
        // Get the current date
        LocalDate currentDate = LocalDate.now();
        System.out.println("Current date: " + currentDate);

        // Get the current time
        LocalTime currentTime = LocalTime.now();
        System.out.println("Current time: " + currentTime);

        // Get the current date and time
        LocalDateTime currentDateTime =
LocalDateTime.now();
        System.out.println("Current date and time: " +
currentDateTime);

        // Create a date
        LocalDate date = LocalDate.of(2023, Month.JANUARY,
26);
        System.out.println("Date: " + date);

        // Add days to a date
        LocalDate datePlusDays = date.plusDays(5);
```

```
        System.out.println("Date plus 5 days: " +
datePlusDays);

        // Subtract months from a date
        LocalDate dateMinusMonths = date.minusMonths(2);
        System.out.println("Date minus 2 months: " +
dateMinusMonths);
    }
}
```

Question 16

How do you compare two dates in Java to check if they are equal?

This is one of the easier questions you will see in terms of skill checking on Date classes. The `java.util.Date` class implements the `equals()` method, which returns `true` if both Dates are the same and `false` otherwise. You can also use the compareTo() method to compare two date objects in Java as shown below:

Here is an example using **equals()** method:

```
Date date1 = new Date();
Date date2 = new Date();
if (date1.equals(date2)) {
    System.out.println("Dates are equal.");
} else {
    System.out.println("Dates are not equal.");
}
```

And here is an example using **compareTo()** method:

```
Date date1 = new Date();
Date date2 = new Date();
if (date1.compareTo(date2) == 0) {
    System.out.println("Dates are equal.");
} else {
    System.out.println("Dates are not equal.");
}
```

In both cases, the **equals()** method and **compareTo()** method will return **true** if the two dates represent the same point in time, and **false** otherwise.

Question 17

How do you find if one date comes before or after another date in Java?

This is the follow-up question to the previous question. The interviewer further checks the candidate's date comparison skill by asking this question. The answer is simple, the `java.util.Date` class provides `before()` and `after()` method, which returns true and false if the date on which the method is called comes before or after the other date passed as a method argument.

Question 18

How do you convert `java.util.Date` to `java.sql.Date` in Java JDBC?

It's the follow-up question to the 6th question. Since `java.sql.Date` is a subclass of `java.util.Date` you can simply get the time in a millisecond and pass it to SQL date as shown below:

```
Date now = new Date();
java.sql.Date sqlDate = new
java.sql.Date(now.getTime());
```

Question 19

How to convert local time to GMT in Java?

To convert local time to GMT in Java, you can use the **java.time** package that was introduced in Java 8.

Here's an example:

```
import java.time.LocalDateTime;
import java.time.ZoneId;
import java.time.ZonedDateTime;
import java.time.format.DateTimeFormatter;


public class TimeZoneExample {
    public static void main(String[] args) {
        // create a LocalDateTime object representing
local time
        LocalDateTime localDateTime =
LocalDateTime.parse("2023-01-27T09:00:00");

        // get the local time zone
        ZoneId localZone = ZoneId.systemDefault();

        // convert local time to GMT
        ZonedDateTime zdt =
localDateTime.atZone(localZone).withZoneSameInstant(Zone
Id.of("GMT"));

        // format the output
        String output =
zdt.format(DateTimeFormatter.ISO_LOCAL_DATE_TIME);

        System.out.println("Local Time: " +
localDateTime);
        System.out.println("GMT Time: " + output);
    }
}
```

In this example, we first create a **LocalDateTime** object representing the local time. We then get the local time zone using the **ZoneId.systemDefault**() method. We use the **atZone**() method to convert the **LocalDateTime** to a **ZonedDateTime** object in the local time zone. Finally, we use the **withZoneSameInstant**() method to convert the **ZonedDateTime** to GMT, and then format the output using **DateTimeFormatter.ISO_LOCAL_DATE_TIME**.

Note that the **java.time** package is thread-safe and provides many other features for working with date and time in Java.

Question 20

What is the difference between `java.util.Date` and `java.sql.Date` in Java?

There are many differences between them, but the most important one is that `java.sql.The date` is from the JDBC package, and it acts as converted between Date and Time data types in the database and Date in Java.

Question 21

How do you calculate the difference between two dates in Java?

There are multiple ways to calculate the difference between two dates in Java, e.g., you can get the long millisecond values from two dates and get the difference, but that's not very valuable; you mostly need the difference in days or hours. See the program to learn more about those differences.

Question 22

How do you convert a string (YYYYMMDD) to date in Java?

You can use `SimpleDateFormat` before JDK 8 and DateTimeFormatter, along with the format and parse method to convert a string to date in Java.

That's all about the frequentlya sked **Date, Time, and Calendar based Java Interview Questions**. A Java developer needs to have a solid understanding of Java's Date and Time API, both old and new because you will not find Java 8 in every project you work on. You still need to know how to work with the old Date and Calendar API while maintaining the legacy project for a couple more years.

CHAPTER 10:
EQUALS AND HASHCODE INTERVIEW QUESTIONS

E quals and HashCode methods in Java are two fundamental methods from java.lang.Object class, which is used to compare the equality of objects, is primarily inside hash-based collections such as `Hashtable` and `HashMap`. Both `equals()` and `hashCode()` are defined in `java.lang.Object` class and their default implementation are based upon Object information, e.g., the default `equals()` method returns true if two objects are exactly the same, i.e., they are pointing to the same memory address, while the default implementation of the hashcode method return `int,` and is implemented as a native method. A similar default implementation of the `toString()` method returns the type of class, followed by the memory address in hex String.

It's advised to `override` these methods based on logical and business rules, e.g., `String` overrides equals to check the equality of two String based upon content. We have also seen the example implementation of `equals()` and hashCode for custom classes. Because of their usefulness and usage, they are also very popular in various levels of Java Interviews, and

In this tutorial, I am going to share some of the really interesting questions from equals() and hashCode() methods in Java. This question not only tests your concept of both methods but also gives you an opportunity to explore them more.

Equals and HashCode Interview Questions in Java

Here is my list of 10 interesting questions on both of these methods. I have seen programmer struggles to write equals() and hashCode() by hand for a rich class, which contains different data types, e.g., int, float, date, etc.

Reading those items and trying examples will give you enough confidence to face any question on equals and hashCode methods. I also suggest reading Effective Java Items on equals() and hashCode() to fill your gaps in knowledge of these two critical methods.

Question 1

When you are writing the equals() method, which other method or methods do you need to override?

Hashcode is the right answer. Since equals and hashCode have their contract, so overriding one and not the other will break the contract between them. By the way, this question can lead to an interesting discussion if the Interviewer likes to go on deep, e.g., he may ask what those contracts are, what happens if those contracts break, etc.

I like to give an example of How equals and hashcode are used in hash-based collections, e.g., Hashtable, which leaves a positive impression more often. You can also mention compareTo() here to score some additional points. This method should also need to be consistent with equals, which is another interesting question on our list.

Question 2

Can two objects which are not equal have the same hashCode?

YES, two objects which are not equal to `equals()` method can still return the same `hashCode`. By the way, this is one of the confusing bits of `equals` and `hashcode` contracts.

Question 3

How does the get() method of HashMap work if two keys have the same hashCode?

This is the follow-up of previous interview questions on equals and hashcode. In fact, sometimes, this leads to a discussion of the earlier point. When two keys return the same `hashcode`, they end up in the same bucket. Now, in order to find the correct value, you use `keys.equals()` method to compare with the key stored in each `Entry` of the linked list there. Remember to point out `keys.equals()` method because that's what the interviewer is looking for.

Question 4

Where have you written equals() and hashCode in your project?

This is to see if the developer has even written these methods or not. Of course, almost all Java programmers are exposed to this. You can point out value objects and Hibernate entities from your domain, where you have overridden equals and hashCode. Always give examples from your domain and from your project rather than a trivial example from a test program because if the Interviewer is asking this question, it means he is interested in examples from your domain.

Question 5

Suppose your Class has an Id field; should you include it in equals()? Why?

This question is asked to one of my readers as Hibernate Interview question, well including id is not a good idea in the equals() method because this method should check equality based upon content and business rules. Also, including id, which is mostly a database identifier and not available to transient objects until they are saved into the database.

Question 6

What happens if equals() is not consistent with the compareTo() method?

This is an interesting question, which is asked along with the `equals()` and `hashCode()` contracts. Some `java.util.Set` implementations, e.g., `SortedSet` or its concrete implementation `TreeSet` uses the `compareTo()` method for comparing objects. If `compareTo()` is not consistent means it doesn't return zero, and if the `equals()` method returns `true`, it may break `Set` contract, **which is not to avoid any duplicates.**

Question 7

What happens if you compare an object to a null using equals()?

When a null object is passed as an argument to the `equals()` method, it should return false, it must not throw `NullPointerException`, but if you call the `equals` method on reference, which is `null`, it will throw NullPointerException. That's why it's better to use the == operator for comparing null, e.g., `if(object != null) object.equals(anohterObject)`. By the way, if you are comparing a `String` literal with another `String` object, then you better call the `equals()` method on the String literal rather than the known object to avoid NPE, one of those simple tricks to avoid `NullPointerException` in Java.

Question 8

What is the difference in using instanceof and getClass() method for checking type inside equals?

This question was asked multiple times, sometimes by looking at your equals() and hashCode implementation. Well, the key difference comes from the point that `instanceof` operator returns true, even if compared with the subclass, e.g., Subclass instanceof Superclass is true, but with `getClass()`, it's false.

By using `getClass()`, you ensure that your `equals()` implementation doesn't return true if compared with the subclass object. While if you use `instanceof` operator, you end up breaking the symmetry rule for equals which says that if `a.equals(b)` is `true`, then `b.equals(a)` should also be `true`. Just replace a and b with an instance of Superclass and Subclass, and you will end up breaking the symmetry rule for the `equals()` method.

Question 9

How do you avoid NullPointerException, while comparing two Strings in Java?

Since when compared to null, equals return false and doesn't throw `NullPointerException`, you can use this property to avoid NPE while using comparing String. Suppose you have a known String `"abc"` and you are comparing with an unknown String variable str, then you should call equals as `"abc".equals(str)`. This will not throw an Exception in thread Main: `java.lang.NullPointerException`, even if str is null.

On the other hand, if you call `str.equals("abc")`, it will throw NPE. So be careful with this. By the way, this is one of the best Java coding practices that Java developers should follow while using the `equals()` method.

Question 10

What is the difference between the "==" and the equals() method in Java?

One of the most classic interview questions on `equals()`. It has been asked numerous times during the past decade and its also one of the basic concept every Java developer should be aware of.

In Java, "==" is a comparison operator used to compare two primitive values or object references to see if they are pointing to the same memory location. On the other hand, the equals() method is a method defined in the Object class and can be overridden by a class to compare the contents of two objects for equality.

When comparing two objects using "==", Java checks whether the two references point to the same memory location. In contrast, when using the equals() method, Java compares the contents of the two objects to check for equality.

It is important to note that the default implementation of the equals() method in the Object class compares the memory location of two objects, similar to the "==" operator. Therefore, if you want to compare the contents of two objects using the equals() method, you need to override the method in the class and provide your own implementation.

That's all on this **list of Java Interview Questions on Equals and HashCode methods in Java.** It's one of the fundamental concepts of Java programming language, but yet it has several subtle things which are unknown to many Java programmers. I strongly suggest getting yourself really good on `equals()`, `hashCode()`, `compareTo()`, and `compare()` methods, not only to do well on Java Interviews but also to write correct code in Java.

CHAPTER 11:
NIO, SOCKET, AND NETWORKING INTERVIEW QUESTIONS

Hello guys, if you are preparing for a Java developer interview, then you may know that Networking and Socket Programming is one of the important areas of Java programming language, especially for those programmers who are working in client server-based applications. Knowledge of important protocols like TCP and UDP in detail is very important, especially if you are in the business of writing high-frequency trading applications which communicate via FIX Protocol or native exchange protocol. In this article, we will discuss some of the *frequently asked questions on networking and socket programming,* mostly based on TCP IP protocol.

This chapter is kinda light on NIO, though, as it doesn't include questions from multiplexing, selectors, `ByteBuffer,` and `FileChannel,` but it does include classical questions like the *difference between IO and NIO.*

The main focus of this post is to make Java developers familiar with low-level parts like how `TCP` and `UDP` protocol works, socket options, and writing multi-threaded servers in Java.

The questions discussed here are not really tied up with Java programming language and can be used in any programming language, which allows programmers to write client-server applications.

By the way, If you are going for an interview on Investment banks for a core Java developer role, you better prepare well on Java NIO, Socket Programming, TCP, UDP, and Networking, along with other popular topics like multi-threading, Collections API, and Garbage Collection tuning. You can also contribute any question which is asked of you or related to socket programming and networking and can be useful for Java interviews.

15 Best Java Networking and Socket Programming Questions with Answers for 3 to 5 Years Experienced Programmers

Here is my list of 15 interview questions related to networking basics, internet protocol, and socket programming in Java. Though it doesn't contain basic questions from APIs like `Server` and `ServerSocket`, it focuses on the high-level concept of writing the scalable server in Java using NIO selectors and how to implement that using threads, their limitations, and issues, etc.

Question 1

What is the difference between TCP and UDP protocol?

There are many differences between TCP (Transmission Control Protocol) and UDP (User Datagram Protocol), but the main is that TCP is connection-oriented, while UDP is connectionless. This means TCP provides guaranteed delivery of messages in the order they are sent, while UDP doesn't provide any delivery guarantee.

Because of this guarantee, **TCP is slower than UDP**, as it needs to perform more work. TCP is best suited for the messages that you can't afford to lose, like order and trade messages in electronic trading, wire transfers in banking and finance, etc. UDP is more suited for media transmission, where the loss of one packet, known as datagrams, is affordable and doesn't affect the quality of service.

This answer is enough for most of the interviews, but you need to be more detailed when you are interviewing as a Java developer for a high-frequency trading desk. Some of the points which many candidates forget to mention are *order* and *data boundary*.

In TCP, messages are guaranteed to be delivered in the same order as they are sent, but data boundary is not preserved, which means multiple messages can be combined and sent together, or the receiver may receive one part of the message in one packet and other parts of the message in next packet.

Though the application will receive the full message in the same order, TCP protocol will do the assembling of the message for you. On the other hand, UDP sends a full message in a datagram packet. If clients receive the packet, it is guaranteed that they will get the full message, but there is no guarantee that the packet will come in the same order they are sent.

In short, you must mention the following differences between TCP and UDP protocols while answering during the interview:

- ➢ TCP is guaranteed delivery, and UDP is not guaranteed.
- ➢ TCP guarantees the order of messages, and UDP doesn't.
- ➢ Data boundary is not preserved in TCP, but UDP preserves it.
- ➢ TCP is slower compared to UDP.

Question 2

How does TCP handshake work?

Three messages are exchanged as part of the TCP head-shake, e.g., Initiator sends SYN. Upon receiving this, Listener sends SYN-ACK, and finally, the initiator replies with ACK. At this point, the TCP connection is moved to the ESTABLISHED state. This process is easily understandable by looking at the following diagram.

Question 3

How do you implement reliable transmission in UDP protocol?

This is usually a follow-up to the previous interview question. Though UDP doesn't provide a delivery guarantee at the protocol level, you can introduce your own logic to maintain reliable messaging, e.g., by introducing sequence numbers and retransmission.

If the receiver finds that it has missed a sequence number, it can ask for a replay of that message from the Server. TRDP protocol, which is used by Tibco Rendezvous (a popular high-speed messaging middleware), uses UDP for faster messaging and provides a reliability guarantee by using sequence numbers and retransmission.

Question 4

What is Network Byte Order? How do two hosts communicate if they have different byte-ordering?

There are two ways to store two bytes in memory, little-endian (least significant byte at the starting address) and big-endian (most significant byte at the starting address). They are collectively known as host byte orders.

For example, an Intel processor stores the 32-bit integer as four consecutive bytes in memory in the order 1-2-3-4, where 1 is the most significant byte.

IBM PowerPC processors would store the integer in the byte order $4-3-2-1$. Networking protocols such as TCP are based on a specific *network byte order*, which uses *big-endian* byte ordering. If two machines are communicating with each other and they have different byte ordering, they are converted to network byte order before sending or after receiving.

Therefore, a little-endian micro-controller sending to a UDP/IP network must swap the order in which bytes appear within multi-byte values before the values are sent onto the network and just swap the order in which bytes appear in multi-byte values received from the network before the values are used. In short, you can also say network byte order is the standard of storing bytes during transmission, and it uses a **big-endian byte ordering mechanism.**

Question 5

What is Nagle's algorithm?

If the interviewer is testing your knowledge of TCP/IP protocol, then it's very rare for him not to ask this question. Nagle's algorithm is a way of improving the performance of TCP/IP protocol and networks by reducing the number of TCP packets that need to be sent over the network. It works by buffering small packets until the buffer reaches Maximum Segment Size.

Small packets, which contain only 1 or 2 bytes of data, have more overhead in terms of the TCP header, which is 40 bytes. These small packets can also lead to congestion in a slow network. Nagle's algorithm tries to improve the efficiency of TCP protocol by buffering them to send a larger packet.

Also, Nagle's algorithm has a negative effect on non-small writes, so if you are writing large data on packets, then it's better to *disable Nagle's algorithm.*

In general, Nagle's algorithm is a defense against careless applications, which send lots of small packets to the network, but it will not benefit or have a negative effect on well-written applications which properly take care of buffering.

Here is also a nice diagram that explains the network traffic with and without Nagle's algorithm:

Question 6

What is TCP_NODELAY?

TCP_NODELAY is an option to disable Nagle's algorithm, provided by various TCP implementations. Since Nagle's algorithm performs badly with the TCP delayed acknowledgment algorithm, it's better to disable Nagle's when you are doing the `write-write-read` operation.

Where a read after two successive writes on the socket may get delayed up to 500 milliseconds until the second write has reached the destination.

If latency is more concerned over bandwidth usage, like in a network-based multi-player game, the user wants to see action from other players immediately. It's better to bypass Nagle's delay by using the `TCP_NODELAY` flag.

Question 7

What is multicasting or multicast transmission? Which Protocol is generally used for multicast? TCP or UDP?

Multi-casting or multicast transmission is one of the too many distributions where the message is delivered to a group of subscribers simultaneously in a single transmission from the publisher. Copies of messages are automatically created in other network elements, e.g., Routers, but only when the topology of a network requires it.

Tibco Rendezvous supports multicast transmission. Multi-casting can only be implemented using UDP because it sends full data as a datagram package, which can be replicated and delivered to other subscribers. Since TCP is a point-to-point protocol, it cannot deliver messages to multiple subscribers until it has a link between each of them.

Though UDP is not reliable, messages may be lost or delivered out of order. Reliable multicast protocols such as Pragmatic General Multicast (PGM) have been developed to add loss detection and retransmission on top of IP multicast.

IP multicast is widely deployed in enterprises, commercial stock exchanges, and multimedia content delivery networks. Common enterprise use of IP multicast is for IPTV applications

Question 8

What is the difference between Topic and Queue in JMS?

The main difference between Topic and Queue in Java Messaging Service is that Queue is used for point-to-point communication, which is generally one-to-one, while the publisher is used for publish and subscribe communication which is one-to-many.

You should use Topic to send messages when we have multiple consumers to consumer messages. If we set up multiple listener threads to consume messages from Queue, each message will be dispatched to only one thread and not all threads. On the other hand, in the case of a Topic, each subscriber gets their own copy of the message.

Question 9

What is the difference between IO and NIO in Java?

The main difference between NIO and IO is that NIO provides asynchronous, non-blocking IO, which is critical to write faster and scalable networking systems. In contrast, most of the utilities from IO classes are blocking and slow.

NIO takes advantage of asynchronous system calls in UNIX systems, such as `select()` system call for network sockets. Using `select()`, an application can monitor several resources at the same time and can also poll network activity without blocking.

The `select()` system call identifies if data is pending or not, then `read()` or `write()` may be used, knowing that they will be complete immediately.

Question 10

How do you write a multi-threaded server in Java?

A multi-threaded server is one that can serve multiple clients without blocking. Java provides excellent support to developers, such as servers. Prior to Java 1.4, you could write a multi-threaded server using traditional socket IO and threads.

This had a severe limitation on scalability because it creates a new thread for each connection, and you can only create a fixed number of threads, depending upon the machine's and platform's capability.

Though this design can be improved by using thread pools and worker threads, it is still a resource-intensive design. After JDK 1.4 and NIO's introduction, writing scalable and multi-threaded servers became a bit easier. You can easily create it in a single thread by using Selector, which takes advantage of the asynchronous and non-blocking IO model of Java NIO.

Question 11

What is the ephemeral port?

In TCP/IP, connection usually contains four things, Server IP, Server port, Client IP, and Client Port. Out of these four, three are well-known most of the time. What is not known is the client port; this is where ephemeral ports come into the picture.

Ephemeral ports are dynamic ports assigned by your machine's IP stack from a specified range, known as the ephemeral port range when a client connection explicitly doesn't specify a port number.

These are short-lived, temporary ports, which can be reused once the connection is closed, but most IP software doesn't reuse ephemeral ports until the whole range is exhausted. Similar to TCP, UDP protocol also uses an ephemeral port while sending the datagram.

In Linux ephemeral port range is from `32768` to `61000`, while in windows default ephemeral port range is 1025 to 5000. The similarly different operating system has different ephemeral port ranges

Question 12

What is the sliding window protocol?

Sliding window protocol is a technique for controlling transmitted data packets between two network computers where reliable and sequential delivery of data packets is required, such as provided by the Transmission Control Protocol (TCP).

In the sliding window technique, each packet includes a unique consecutive sequence number, which is used by the receiving computer to place data in the correct order. The objective of the sliding window technique is to use the sequence numbers to avoid duplicate data and to request missing data

Question 13

When do you get the "too many files open" error?

Just like File connection, Socket Connection also needs file descriptors. Since every machine has a limited number of file descriptors, it's possible that they may run out of file descriptors. When it happens, you will see a *"too many files open"* error. You can check how many file descriptor per process is allowed on

UNIX based system by executing the `ulimit  -n` command or simply counting entries on `/proc//fd/`

Question 14

What is the TIME_WAIT state in TCP protocol? When does a socket connection go to the TIME_WAIT state?

When one end of the TCP Connection closes it by making a system call, it goes into the TIME_WAIT state. Since TCP packets can arrive in the wrong order, the port must not be closed immediately to allow late packets to arrive. That's why that end of the TCP connection goes into the TIME_WAIT state.

For example, if a client closes a socket connection, then it will go to the `TIME_WAIT` state. Similarly, if the server closes the connection, then you will see `TIME_WAIT` there. You can check the status of your TCP and UDP sockets by using these networking commands in UNIX.

Question 15

What will happen if you have too many socket connections in the TIME_WAIT state on the Server?

When a socket connection or port goes into the `TIME_WAIT` state, it doesn't release the file descriptor associated with it. The file descriptor is only released when the `TIME_WAIT` state is gone, i.e., after some specified configured time. If too many connections are in the `TIME_WAIT` state, then your Server may run out of file descriptors and start throwing a *"too many files open"* error, and stop accepting new connections.

That's all about in this list of **networking and socket programming interview questions and answers**. Though I originally intended this list for Java programmers, it is equally useful for any programmer.

In fact, this is the bare minimum knowledge of sockets and protocols every programmer should have. I have found that C and C++ programmers are better at answering these questions than the average Java programmers.

One reason for this may be because Java programmers have got so many useful libraries like Apache MINA, which does all the low-level work for them. Anyway, knowledge of fundamentals is very important, and everything else is just an excuse, but at some point, I also recommend using tried and tested libraries like Apache MINA for production code.

CHAPTER 12:
JAVA WEB SERVICE INTERVIEW QUESTIONS

W eb Services interview questions are part of J2EE interviews for jobs that are looking for some experience in the Java web services Space. Most of the Web services questions come from two different ways of implementing Web Services like SOAP and REST. SOAP is a standard and mature way of calling Web Services, which uses XML, while REST is a new way of implementing Web Services, which is based on HTTP protocol. In fact, REST Web Service interview questions are getting more and more popular in web services interviews in Java, So if you are going for any Java J2EE interview which requires some web service experience, be prepared with both SOAP and REST Web services questions.

Following is a list of *Java web services interview questions* that I have prepared for practice. Answers to these web services questions can be easily found in many places on the Internet, and I will update this list whenever I have new web services interview questions.

20 Frequently asked Java web services interview questions

Here is my list of frequently asked interview questions on the Java web service in any Core Java Interview. As SOAP is a standard way of making web service call that uses XML, good knowledge of XML and Java is expected from you, and Interviewer may ask some *XML interview questions* as well.

Question 1

What is Web Service?

It's like a website where you send requests and receive responses, but unlike traditional websites where you receive HTML responses, web services generally respond with JSON or XML. In today's world web services implements API, client call them and server return response in JSON.

Question 2

What is SOAP?

It's a technology to implement web services. SOAP stands for Simple Object Access Protocol which is a messaging protocol that allows distributed elements of an application to communicate. SOAP can be carried over a variety of lower-level protocols, including the web-related Hypertext Transfer Protocol (HTTP).

Question 3

What is REST Web Service?

REST is a short form of REpresentational State Transfer. It's another way to implement web services, and it's also quite popular these days. It uses HTTP protocol and its various methods instead of a separate protocol to convey information. For example, GET can retrieve data, and POST can create data on a REST web service.

Question 4

What is the difference between REST Web Service and SOAP web service?

REST (Representational State Transfer) and SOAP (Simple Object Access Protocol) are two different web service architectures used for communication between different software applications.

The main differences between REST and SOAP web services are as follows:

1. Protocol: REST web services use HTTP (Hypertext Transfer Protocol) protocol for communication while SOAP web services can use any protocol such as HTTP, SMTP, TCP, or UDP.

2. Messaging: In REST web services, messages are usually sent and received in JSON or XML format, while in SOAP web services, messages are typically sent and received in XML format.

3. Data format: REST web services use simple data formats such as JSON or XML, while SOAP web services use a more complex data format that can include type information, metadata, and error details.

4. Ease of use: REST web services are generally easier to use and understand than SOAP web services because they use simple data formats and rely on HTTP's built-in features.

5. Scalability: REST web services are more scalable than SOAP web services because they are stateless and require less bandwidth.

Overall, REST web services are lightweight, simple, and flexible, while SOAP web services are powerful, complex, and rigid. The choice of architecture depends on the specific needs and requirements of the application. REST is also an architectural-style protocol, unlike SOAP which is an XML-based protocol. Also, SOAP is invoked using the RPC method, while REST web services can be simply called using a URL path.

Question 5

Can a Java client talk to C++ Server using Web Service?

Yes, the main advantage of web services is that the client and server can be implemented on different technologies or programming languages. They can also be independently development. Since they communicate over XML or JSON, which is intended by any tech to transfer messages or data, you can create a Java client to talk to a C++ server.

Question 6

What is WSDL?

WSDL stands for Web Service Description language, and it is used to describe the services offered by any web service. In the case of SOAP-based web service, you can find all the functions you can call in their WSDL document.

Question 7

What is UDDI?

UDDI stands for Universal Description, Discovery, and Integration. It's an open specification that **defines a way to publish and discover information about Web services**. UDDI has two functions: In the case of a SOAP-based protocol, it defines how clients communicate with UDDI registries, and it also contains a particular set of globally replicated registries where anyone can register their web service.

Question 8

Is Web Service call synchronous or asynchronous?

It could be both, but generally, asynchronous web service calls are preferred because the client doesn't need to wait for the response. It can asynchronously process the response when it receives it and continues doing its work.

Question 9

How do you handle errors in Web Service calls?

In web service calls, errors can be handled in several ways:

1. Try-Catch Block:
   you can use try-catch block to handle exceptions thrown during the web service call. This can be used to handle specific exceptions and perform different actions based on the type of exception.

2. Response Status Code:
   you can also check the response status code to determine if the web service call was successful or not. A status code of 200 indicates a successful call, while other status codes indicate errors.

3. Error Response Message:
   Check the error response message returned by the web service to get more information about the error. This can be used to provide more detailed error messages to the user.

4. Logging:
   You should log the error messages to help with debugging and troubleshooting. This can be especially useful when errors occur in a production environment.

5. Retrying:
   You should retry the web service call if it fails due to a transient error. This can be done by catching the exception and retrying the call a certain number of times before giving up.

6. Circuit Breaker:
   You can also use a circuit breaker pattern to detect when a web service is not responding and prevent further requests from being sent until the service is available again.

Question 10

What is JAX-RPC?

JAX-RPC is a Java specification that defines the Java APIs for making XML-based remote procedure calls (RPC). It's an essential library for calling SOAP web services from Java applications.

Question 11

Have you worked on Spring and Web services?

You can answer this question based on your experience. Just be prepared if you answer yes, then questions related to how to call a web service using spring may be asked. If they are RESTful web srvices then you can use RestTemplate or WebClient class to call them. Both these classes allows you to send GET, PUT, POST, and DELTE request to any RESTful Web services over HTTP.

Question 12

What is `WebServiceTemplate` etc.?

Similar to `RestTemplate` and `WebClient`, the `WebServiceTemplate` is the core class for client-side Web service access in Spring-WS. It contains methods for sending Source objects and receiving response messages as either Source or Result.

Question 13

What is the difference between RMI and Web Services?

RMI (Remote Method Invocation) and Web Services are two different technologies used for distributed computing in Java.

RMI is a Java API used for invoking methods remotely between two Java Virtual Machines (JVMs) over the network. It allows Java objects to be invoked remotely and is suitable for Java-to-Java communication within an organization.

On the other hand, Web Services are a standardized way of communication between different platforms, languages, and devices over the internet. They use XML (Extensible Markup Language) and HTTP (Hypertext Transfer Protocol) to transfer data and can be used by any client or server supporting the HTTP protocol. Web Services can be implemented in a variety of languages and platforms, including Java.

The main differences between RMI and Web Services are:

1. Platform Independence: Web Services are platform-independent, whereas RMI is limited to Java-to-Java communication.

2. Standardization: Web Services are standardized using protocols like SOAP (Simple Object Access Protocol) and REST (Representational State Transfer), whereas RMI is a proprietary Java API.

3. Interoperability: Web Services can communicate with any platform or language that supports HTTP, whereas RMI is limited to Java-to-Java communication.

4. Protocol: Web Services use XML and HTTP for communication, whereas RMI uses Java serialization and TCP/IP.

5. Complexity: RMI is generally considered more complex than Web Services, which are easier to implement and use.

In summary, Web Services are a more flexible and interoperable solution for distributed computing over the internet, while RMI is more suitable for Java-to-Java communication within a closed system.

Question 14

What is gRPC? What benefits it offers over other Web service Alternatives?

gRPC is a high-performance, open-source framework for building remote procedure call (RPC) services. It uses Protocol Buffers as its interface definition language (IDL) and provides features such as bi-directional streaming and flow control, among others.

Compared to other web service alternatives like REST or SOAP, gRPC offers several benefits, such as:

1. Efficiency: gRPC uses a binary protocol that is more compact and efficient than text-based protocols like REST or SOAP.

2. Flexibility: gRPC supports multiple programming languages, making it easy to use with a wide range of programming stacks.

3. Streaming: gRPC supports bi-directional streaming, allowing clients and servers to send and receive multiple messages in parallel.

4. Code Generation: gRPC provides code generation for both clients and servers, making it easier to build and maintain RPC services.

5. Interoperability: gRPC allows communication between services written in different programming languages, making it easy to integrate with existing systems.

Question 15

What is Microservice Architecture?

Microservices architecture is a Sofware Development Life Cycle (SDLC) approach in which huge applications are built as a collection of small functional modules. These modules are deployed independently. They are scalable and can communicate with each other over standard protocols, and most importantly, they are loosely coupled. Microservices communicate with each other through APIs and use lightweight protocols, such as HTTP or messaging, to communicate. This architecture allows for greater flexibility, scalability, and resilience in large and complex applications, as well as faster development and deployment cycles.

Question 16

What is the difference between REST and Microservice?

REST is a technology to communicate over HTTP. It allows you to post data to the server and retrieve data from the server using HTTP methods like POST and GET, while Microservices is an architecture pattern where a system is built by creating multiple small services which do one job well. This allows faster development as multiple people can work on different services simultaneously. They are also easy to release and maintain

Question 17

What is the difference between the POST and PUT on REST Web Service?

In REST web service, **POST is used to create a new entity**, while PUT is used to update the existing entity on the server. For example, you can create a new book on a BookService using POST, but if you want to update any attribute of the book, like Title, then you can use the PUT method. But this difference is by convention only. If your server implements it in a different way, then POST and PUT methods will behave accordingly.

Question 18

What is the purpose of different HTTP methods in REST?

POST is mainly used to create data, GET is to retrieve data, PUT is to update data, and DELETE is to remove data on the server.

Question 19

How do you test REST web services?

You can test REST Web Service using tools like `Postman` or just by using the `curl` command in Linux. You can also call them by putting the URL into the browser, and you can see the JSON or XML returned on the browser itself.

Question 20

What is the difference between REST and GraphQL?

While both REST and GraphQL are technology to post and get the data from the server, one major difference is that GraphQL optimizes what REST does. It provides a structure that allows you to query multiple data from different endpoints together, which means you need to make fewer calls to the server. For example, to get both User and Order data using REST will require two queries, one to the user endpoint and the other to the Order endpoint, but with GraphQL, you can get both these data in just one query.

That's all about some **common Java Web Service Interview Questions,** which you can practice before interviews. I have tried to cover all kinds of web services like SOAP, REST, GraphQL, and gRPC so that you have a broad idea about different kinds of web services. You can go through these questions before your Java interview to revise key concepts.

CHAPTER 13:

JAVA EXCEPTION AND ERROR INTERVIEW QUESTIONS

Y ou will always see some interview questions from Exception and Error handling in core Java Interviews. Exception handling is an important aspect of Java application development, and its key to writing robust, stable Java programs, which makes it a natural favorite in interviews. Questions from Error and Exception in Java are mostly based on the concept of Exception and Error in Java, How to handle Exception, best practices to follow during Exception handling, etc. Though multithreading, garbage collection, JVM concepts, and questions from object-oriented design rules these interviews, you should always expect and prepare some questions on effective error handling.

Some Interviewers also test the debugging skill of programmers, as quickly resolving Exceptions is another trait of solid Java programming knowledge.

If the programmer is familiar with the infamous and dodgy `ClassNotFoundException` or `OutOfMemoryError`, there is a good chance that he has some good practical experience under his belt.

In this article, we will see some Java Error and Exception interview questions asked to fresher, experienced, and senior Java developers in Java developer interviews.

Java Exception and Error Interview Questions

Here is my list of frequently asked questions from Java Error and Exception topics in various programming interviews with Java developers. I have also shared my answers to these questions for quick revision and provided the source for a more in-depth understanding.

I have tried to include questions of various difficulty levels, including the simplest of simple for freshers and some tricky questions for senior Java developers.

Question 1

What is an Exception in Java?

This is always the first interview question on Exception and is mostly asked in fresher-level interviews. I haven't seen anybody asking about what exception is in senior and experienced-level interviews, but this is quite popular at the entry level. In simple words, Exception is Java's way of conveying both system and programming errors.

In Java, the Exception feature is implemented by using a class like `Throwable`, `Exception`, `RuntimeException,` and keywords like `throw`, `throws`, `try`, `catch`, and `finally`. All Exceptions are derived from the `Throwable` class.

Throwable further divides errors into two categories. One is `java.lang.Exception` and other is `java.lang.Error`.

`java.lang.Error` deals with system errors like `java.lang.StackOver FlowError` or `Java.lang.OutOfMemoryError` while Exception is mostly used to deal with programming mistakes, non-availability of requested resources, etc.

Question 2

What is the difference between Checked and Unchecked Exceptions in Java?

This is another popular Java Exception interview question that appears in almost all levels of Java interviews. The main difference between Checked and Unchecked Exceptions lies in there handling. Checked Exception requires to be handled at compile time using `try`, `catch`, and `finally`, keywords, or else the compiler will flag the error. This is not a requirement for Unchecked Exceptions. Also, all exceptions are derived from `java.lang.Exception` classes are checked exception, exception those which extends `RuntimeException;` these are known as an unchecked exception in Java

Question 3

What is the similarity between NullPointerException and ArrayIndexOut OfBoundException in Java?

This Java Exception interview question was not very popular but appeared in various fresher-level interviews to see whether the candidate was familiar with the concept of checked and unchecked exceptions or not. By the way answer to this interview question is both of them are an example of unchecked exceptions derived from `RuntimeException`. This question also opens the door for the difference between arrays in Java and C programming language, as arrays in C are unbounded and never throw `ArrayIndexOutOfBoundException`.

Question 4

What best practices do you follow while doing Exception handling in Java?

This Exception interview question in Java is very popular when hiring a senior java developer or Technical Lead. Since exception handling is a crucial part of project design and good knowledge of this is desirable. There are a lot of best practices that can help to make your code robust and flexible at the same time. Here are a few of them:

1. Returning boolean instead of returning null to avoid NullPointerException at callers end. Since NPE is the most infamous of all Java exceptions, there are a lot of techniques and coding best practices to minimize NullPointerException.

2. Non-empty catch blocks. Empty catch blocks are considered as one of the bad practices in Exception handling because they just ate Exceptions without any clue. At the bare minimum, print stack trace, but you should do an alternative operation that makes sense or is defined by requirements.

3. Prefer Unchecked exception over checked until you have a very good reason not to do so. It improves the readability of code by removing boilerplate exception-handling code

4. Never let your database Exception flow till client error. Since most of the application deal with databases and SQLException is a checked Exception in Java, you should consider handling any database-related errors in the DAO layer of your application and only returning an alternative value or something meaningful `RuntimeException` that that which client can understand and take action.

5. Calling `close()` methods for connections, statements, and streams on the final block in Java.

Question 5

Why do you think Checked Exception exists in Java since we can also convey errors using RuntimeException?

This is a controversial question, and you need to be careful while answering this interview question. Though they will definitely like to hear your opinion, what they are most interested in is the convincing reason. One of the reasons I see is that it is a design decision that is influenced by experience in programming languages prior to Java, like C++.

Most of the checked exceptions are in the `java.io` package, which makes sense because if you request any system resource and it's not available, then a robust program must be able to handle that situation gracefully. By declaring `IOException` as a checked Exception, Java ensures that you provide that gracefully exception handling.

Another possible reason could be to ensure that system resources like file descriptors, which are limited in numbers, should be released as soon as you are done with that using catch or finally block. Effective Java book from Joshua Bloch has a couple of items on this topic, which is again worth reading.

Question 6

What is the difference between the throw and throws keywords in Java?

One more Java Exception interview question from beginner's kitty. `throw` and `throws` keyword may look quite similar, especially if you are new to Java programming and haven't seen much of it. Though they are similar in terms of both being used in Exception handling, they are different in how and where they are used in code. The `throws` keyword is used in the method signature to declare which checked exception method can throw. You can also declare unchecked exceptions, but that is not mandatory by the compiler.

This signifies a lot of things, like the method is not going to handle an Exception; instead, it's throwing it. If the method throws a checked Exception, then the caller should provide compile-time exception handling, etc.

On the other hand, the `throw` keyword is actually used to throw any Exception. Syntactically you can throw any Throwable (i.e., `Throwable` or any class derived from `Throwable`); the `throw` keyword transfers control of execution to the caller so it can be used in place of the return keyword. The most common example of using throw in place of return is throwing `UnSupportedOperationException` from an empty method, as shown below :

```
private static void show() {
    throw new UnsupportedOperationException("Not yet
implemented");
}
```

Question 7

What is Exception chaining in Java?

Exception chaining is a popular exception-handling concept in Java, where another exception is thrown in response to an exception and creates a chain of Exceptions. This technique is mostly used to wrap a checked exception into an unchecked or `RuntimeException`. By the way, if you are throwing a new exception due to another exception, then always include the original exception so that the handler code can access the root cause by using methods like `getCause()` and `initCause()`.

Question 8

Have you written your own custom Exception in Java? How do you do that?

Of course, most of us have written custom or business Exceptions like **AccountNotFoundExcepiton**. The main purpose of asking this Java

Exception interview question is to find out how you use this feature. This can be used for sophisticated and precise exception handling with tweaks involved in whether you would choose a checked or unchecked exception.

By creating a specific exception for the specific case, you also give a lot of options to the caller to deal with them elegantly. I always prefer to have a precise exception than a general exception. Though creating lots of specific exceptions increases the number of classes in your project quickly, maintaining a practical balance between specific and general exceptions is key to success.

Question 9

What changes have been introduced in JDK7 related to Exception handling in Java?

JDK7 has introduced two major features which are related to Error and Exception handling. One is the ability to handle multiple exceptions in one catch block, popularly known as multi-cache block, and the other is ARM blocks in Java 7 for automatic resource management, also known as to try with the resource.

Both of these features can certainly help to reduce boilerplate code required for handling checked exceptions in Java and significantly improve the readability of code. Knowledge of this feature not only helps to write better errors and exception code in Java but also helps to do well during interviews. I also recommend reading Java 7 Recipes book to get more insight into useful features introduced in Java 7, including these two.

Question 10

Have you faced OutOfMemoryError in Java? How did you solve that?

This Java Error interview question is mostly asked in senior-level Java interviews, and here the interviewer is interested in your approach to tackling dangerous OutOfMemoryError. Admit it; we always face this error no matter which kind of project you are working on, so if you say no, it doesn't go very well with the interviewer. I suggest even if you are not familiar with facing it in reality but have 3 to 4 years of experience in Java, be prepared for it.

At the same time, this is also a chance to impress the interviewer by showing your advanced technical knowledge related to finding memory leaks, profiling, and debugging.

Question 11

Does code form finally execute if the method returns before finally blocking or JVM exits?

This Java exception interview question can also be asked in code format, where given a code with `System.exit()` in the try block and something in the finally block. It's worth knowing that, finally block in Java executes even when the return keyword is used in the try block. The only time they don't execute is when you call JVM to exit by executing `System.exit(0)` from try block in Java.

Question 12

What is the difference between the final, finalize, and finally keywords in Java?

Another classic interview question in core Java was asked by one of my friends on his telephone interview for a core Java developer with Morgan Stanley. `final` and `finally` are keywords, while `finalize` is a method. The final keyword is very useful for creating an ad Immutable class in Java. By making a class final, we prevent it from being extended. Similarly, by making a method final, we prevent it from being overridden. On the other hand, `finalize()` method is called by the garbage collector before that object is collected, but this is not guaranteed by Java specification. `finally` keyword is the only one which is related to error and exception handling, and you should always have finally block in the production code for closing connections and resources.

Question 13

What is wrong with the following code :

```
public static void start() throws IOException,
RuntimeException{
throw new RuntimeException("Not able to Start");
}

public static void main(String args[]) {
try {
start();
} catch (Exception ex) {
ex.printStackTrace();
} catch (RuntimeException re) {
re.printStackTrace();
}
}
```

This code will throw a compiler error on the line where the RuntimeException variable "re" is written on the catch block. Since Exception is a superclass of RuntimeException, all RuntimeException thrown by the start() method will be captured by the first catch block, and code will never reach the second catch block, and that's the reason the compiler will flag error as *"exception* java.lang.RuntimeException *has already been caught"*.

Question 14

What is wrong with the following code in Java:

```
public class SuperClass {
  public void start() throws IOException{
```

```
      throw new IOException("Not able to open file");
   }
 }

  public class SubClass extends SuperClass{
  public void start() throws Exception{
    throw new Exception("Not able to start");
  }
}
```

In this code, the compiler will complain about the subclass where the start() method gets overridden. As per the rules of method overriding in Java, an overridden method can not throw a Checked Exception, which is higher in the hierarchy than the original method. Since here start() is throwing IOException in the superclass, start() in the subclass can only throw either IOException or any subclass of IOException but not the superclass of IOException, e.g., Exception.

Question 15

What is wrong with the following Java Exception code:

```
public static void start(){
   System.out.println("Java Exception interivew
question Answers for Programmers");
}

public static void main(String args[]) {
   try{
     start();
  }catch(IOException ioe){
  ioe.printStackTrace();
  }
}
```

In this Java Exception example code, the compiler will complain about the line where we are handling `IOException`; since `IOException` is a checked Exception and the `start()` method doesn't throw `IOException`, the compiler will flag the error as `"exception java.io.IOException is never thrown in body of corresponding try statement,"` but if you change `IOException` to Exception compiler error will disappear because Exception can be used to catch all `RuntimeException` which doesn't require a declaration in a throws clause.

I like this little tricky Java Exception interview question because it's not easy to figure out the result by chaining `IOException` to `Exception`. You can also check Java Puzzlers by Joshua Bloch and Neil Gafter for some tricky questions based on Java Errors and Exceptions.

These are some of the Java Error and Exception interview questions I have mostly seen in both fresher and experienced levels of Java interviews. There are a lot more questions on Exception that I haven't included, and if you think you have a good question missed out, then let me know, and I will make an effort to include it on this list of java exceptions questions and answers.

One last question about Java Exception I am leaving for you guys is "Why is Java Exception considered to be a better alternative for returning error codes"? Ponder this question as its thought-provoking

CHAPTER 14:
TRICKY JAVA INTERVIEW QUESTIONS

What is a tricky question? Well, tricky Java interview questions are those questions that have some surprise element to them. If you try to answer a tricky question with common sense, you will most likely fail because they require some specific knowledge. Most of the tricky Java questions come from confusing concepts like method overloading and overriding, Multi-threading, which is really tricky to master character encoding, checked vs. unchecked exceptions, and subtle Java programming details like Integer overflow. The most important thing to answer a tricky Java question is attitude and analytical thinking, which helps even if you don't know the answer.

Anyway, in this Java article, we will see 10 Java questions that are really tricky and requires more than average knowledge of Java programming language to answer correctly. As per my experience, there are always one or two tricky or tough Java interview questions on any core Java or Java EE interviews, so it's good to prepare tricky questions from Java in advance.

If I take an interview, I purposefully put this kind of question to gauge the depth of the candidate's understanding of Java. Another advantage of asking such a question is the surprising element, which is a key factor in putting the candidate under some pressure during interviews.

Since these questions are less common, there is a good chance that many Java developer doesn't know about them. You won't find these questions even on popular Java interview courses like the **Java Interview Guide: 200+ Interview Questions and Answers**, which is nevertheless an excellent guide for Java interviews.

10 Tricky Java interview questions - Answered.

Here is my list of 10 tricky Java interview questions. Though I have prepared and shared a lot of difficult core Java interview questions and answers, I have chosen them as the Top 10 tricky questions because you can not guess answers to these tricky Java questions easily. You need some subtle details of Java programming language to answer these questions.

Question 1

Question: **What does the following Java program print?**

```
public class Test {
  public static void main(String[] args) {
    System.out.println(Math.min(Double.MIN_VALUE,
0.0d));
  }
}
```

This question is tricky because unlike the Integer, where MIN_VALUE is negative, both the MAX_VALUE and MIN_VALUE of the Double class are positive numbers. The Double.MIN_VALUE is $2^{(-1074)}$, a double constant whose magnitude is the least among all double values.

So unlike the obvious answer, *this program will print 0.0* because of `Double.MIN_VALUE` is greater than 0. I have asked this question to a Java developer having experience of up to 3 to 5 years, and surprisingly almost 70% of candidates got it wrong.

Question 2

What will happen if you put the return statement or System.exit () on the try or catch block? Will finally block execute?

This is a very popular tricky Java question, and it's tricky because many programmers think that no matter what, the finally block will always execute. This question challenges that concept by putting a return statement in the try or catch block or calling `System.exit()` from the try or catch block.

The answer to this tricky question in Java is that finally, the block will execute even if you put a return statement in the try block or catch block, but finally block won't run if you call `System.exit()` from the try or catch block.

Question 3

Can you override a private or static method in Java?

This is another popular Java tricky question. As I said, method overriding is a good topic to ask trick questions in Java. Anyway, you can not override a private or static method in Java; if you create a similar method with the same return type and the same method arguments in the child class, then it will hide the superclass method. This is known as method hiding.

Similarly, you cannot override a private method in the subclass because it's not accessible there. What you do is create another private method with the same name in the child class.

Question 4

What will the expression 1.0 / 0.0 return? Will it throw an Exception? Any compile-time error?

This is another tricky question from the Double class. Though Java developers know about the double primitive type and Double class, while doing floating-point arithmetic, they don't pay enough attention to `Double.INFINITY`, NaN, and `-0.0` and other rules that govern the arithmetic calculations involving them.

The simple answer to this question is that it will not throw `ArithmeticExcpetion` and return `Double.INFINITY`.

Also, note that the comparison `x == Double.NaN` always evaluates to false, even if x itself is a NaN. To test if x is a NaN, one should use the method called `Double.isNaN(x)` to check if the given number is NaN or not. If you know SQL, this is very close to NULL there.

Question 5

Does Java support multiple inheritances?

This is the trickiest question in Java; if C++ can support direct multiple inheritances, then why not Java? This is the argument Interviewer often gives. The answer to this question is much more subtle than it looks because Java does support multiple inheritances of Type by allowing an interface to extend other interfaces. What Java doesn't support is multiple inheritances of implementation.

This distinction also gets blurred because of the default method of Java 8, which now provides Java multiple inheritances of behavior as well.

Question 6

What will happen if we put a key object in a HashMap which is already there?

This tricky Java question is part of another frequently asked question, How HashMap works in Java. HashMap is also a popular topic for creating confusing and tricky questions in Java.

The answer to this question is if you put the same key again, then it will replace the old mapping because HashMap doesn't allow duplicate keys. The Same key will result in the same hashcode and will end up at the same position in the bucket.

Each bucket contains a linked list of `Map.Entry` object, which contains both Key and Value. Now Java will take the Key object from each entry and compare it with this new key using the `equals()` method. If that returns true, then the value object in that entry will be replaced by the new value.

Question 7

What does the following Java program print?

```java
public class Test {
  public static void main(String[] args) throws Exception
  {
    char[] chars = new char[] {'\u0097'};
    String str = new String(chars);
    byte[] bytes = str.getBytes();
    System.out.println(Arrays.toString(bytes));
  }
}
```

The trickiness of this question lies in character encoding and how String to byte array conversion works. In this program, we are first creating a String from a character array, which just has one character `'\u0097'`. After that, we get the byte array from that String and print that byte.

Since \u0097 is within the 8-bit range of byte primitive type, it is reasonable to guess that the str.getBytes() call will return a byte array that contains one element with a value of -105 ((byte) 0x97).

However, that's not what the program prints, and that's why this question is tricky. As a matter of fact, the output of the program is operating system and locale-dependent on a Windows XP with the US locale, the above program prints [63]. If you run this program on Linux or Solaris, you will get different values.

To answer this question correctly, you need to know about how Unicode characters are represented in Java char values and in Java strings and what role character encoding plays in String.getBytes().

In simple words, to convert a string to a byte array, Java iterates through all the characters that the string represents and turns each one into a number of bytes, and finally puts the bytes together. The rule that maps each Unicode character into a byte array is called character encoding.

So It's possible that if the same character encoding is not used during both encoding and decoding, then the retrieved value may not be correct. When we call str.getBytes() without specifying a character encoding scheme, the JVM uses the default character encoding of the platform to do the job.

The default encoding scheme is an operating system and locale-dependent. On Linux, it is UTF-8, and on Windows, with a US locale, the default encoding is Cp1252. This explains the output we get from running this program on Windows machines with a US locale.

No matter which character encoding scheme is used, Java will always translate Unicode characters not recognized by the encoding to 63, which represents the character U+003F (the question mark, ?) in all encodings.

Question 8

If a method throws NullPointerException in the superclass, can we override it with a method that throws RuntimeException?

One more tricky Java question from the overloading and overriding concept. The answer is you can very well throw a superclass of RuntimeException in overridden method, but you can not do the same if it's a checked Exception.

Question 9

What is the issue with the following implementation of the compareTo() method in Java, where an id is an integer number?

```
public int compareTo(Object o){
   Employee emp = (Employee) o;
     return this.id - e.id;
}
```

Well, there is nothing wrong with this Java question until you guarantee that the id is always positive. This Java question becomes tricky when you can't guarantee that the id is positive or negative. The tricky part is If the id becomes negative, then **subtraction may overflow** and produce an incorrect result.

Question 10

How do you ensure that the N thread can access N resources without deadlock?

If you are not well versed in writing multi-threading code, then this is a really tricky question for you. This Java question can be tricky even for experienced and senior programmers, who are not really exposed to deadlock and race conditions.

The key point here is ordering. If you acquire resources in a particular order and release resources in the reverse order, you can prevent deadlock.

Question 11

Consider the following Java code snippet, which is initializing two variables, and both are not volatile, and two threads T1 and T2, are modifying these values as follows; both are not synchronized

```
int x = 0;
boolean bExit = false;

Thread 1 (not synchronized)
x = 1;
bExit = true;

Thread 2 (not synchronized)
if (bExit == true)
System.out.println("x=" + x);
```

Now tell us, is it possible for Thread 2 to print "x=0"?

It's impossible for a list of tricky Java questions not to contain anything from multi-threading. This is the simplest one I can get. The answer to this question is Yes, and It's possible that thread T2 may print x=0. Why? Because without any instruction to the compiler, e.g., synchronized or volatile, `bExit=true` might come before x=1 in compiler reordering. Also, x=1 might not become visible in Thread 2, so Thread 2 will load x=0. Now, how do you fix it?

When I asked this question to a couple of programmers, they answered differently; one suggested making both threads synchronized on a common mutex, and another one said to make both variables volatile. Both are correct, as they will prevent reordering and guarantee visibility.

But the best answer is you just need to make `bExit` as volatile, and then Thread 2 can only print "x=1". x does not need to be volatile because x cannot be reordered to come after `bExit=true` when `bExit` is volatile.

Question 12

What is the difference between CyclicBarrier and CountDownLatch in Java?

Relatively newer Java tricky question, only been introduced from Java 5. The main difference between both is that you can reuse CyclicBarrier even if the Barrier is broken, but you cannot reuse CountDownLatch in Java.

CyclicBarrier is used when a group of threads need to wait for each other to reach a certain point of execution before proceeding further. It works by allowing a fixed number of threads to wait for each other at a barrier point until all of them reach there. Once all threads have arrived, the barrier is released, and the threads can continue their execution. CyclicBarrier can be reset and reused, making it suitable for recurring synchronization tasks.

On the other hand, CountDownLatch is used when one or more threads need to wait for a specific number of events to occur before proceeding further. It works by initializing a latch with a count, and the threads wait until the count reaches zero. Each time an event occurs, the count is decremented until it reaches zero, and the threads can continue their execution. Unlike CyclicBarrier, CountDownLatch cannot be reset and reused once it has been counted down to zero.

In summary, CyclicBarrier is used for synchronization among a fixed number of threads at a particular barrier point, while CountDownLatch is used for synchronization when one or more threads need to wait for a specific number of events to occur before proceeding.

Question 13

What is the difference between StringBuffer and StringBuilder in Java?

Classic Java questions which some people think are tricky and some consider very easy. StringBuilder in Java was introduced in JDK 1.5, and the only difference between both is that StringBuffer methods like length(), capacity(), or append() are synchronized, while corresponding methods in StringBuilder are not synchronized.

Because of this fundamental difference, the concatenation of String using StringBuilder is faster than StringBuffer. Actually, it's considered a bad practice to use StringBuffer anymore because, in almost 99% of scenarios, you perform string concatenation on the same thread. See StringBuilder vs. StringBuffer for more differences.

Question 14

Can you access a non-static variable in the static context?

Another tricky Java question from Java fundamentals. No, you cannot access a non-static variable from the static context in Java. If you try, it will give a compile-time error. This is actually a common problem for beginners in Java to face when they try to access instance variables inside the main method.

Because the main is static in Java, and instance variables are non-static, you can not access the instance variable inside the main.

Question 15

How many String objects are created by the following code?

You might be thinking of "one" object, but that's wrong. Btw, if you don't find these questions tricky enough, then you should check Joshua Bloch's other classic book, Java Puzzlers, for super tricky questions. I am sure you will find them challenging enough.

More Trick Java Questions for Practice?

Now, it's practice time. Here are some questions for you guys to answer:

1. When doesn't Singleton remain Singleton in Java?

Singleton is a design pattern in Java that restricts the instantiation of a class to only one object. It is a widely used pattern in Java programming as it ensures that a class has only one instance at any given time, and provides a global point of access to that instance.

However, there are certain scenarios in Java where Singleton does not remain Singleton. One such scenario is when multiple classloaders are involved. Each classloader creates its own instance of the Singleton class, resulting in multiple instances of the Singleton class in the memory.

Another scenario where Singleton does not remain Singleton is when serialization and deserialization are involved. When a Singleton class is serialized and then deserialized, a new instance of the Singleton class is created.

Furthermore, when reflection is used to access the private constructor of a Singleton class, it can create new instances of the Singleton class, resulting in multiple instances of the class in the memory.

Therefore, it is important to consider these scenarios while implementing the Singleton pattern in Java to ensure that it remains Singleton.

2. Is it possible to load a class with two ClassLoaders?

Yes, it is possible to load a class with two ClassLoaders in Java. This is known as ClassLoader hierarchy or ClassLoader delegation model. When a class is loaded by a ClassLoader, it delegates the class loading to its parent ClassLoader. If the parent ClassLoader is unable to load the class, then the child ClassLoader loads the class.

In some cases, it may be necessary to load a class with a specific ClassLoader rather than the default system ClassLoader. In such cases, a custom ClassLoader can be created to load the class.

However, loading a class with multiple ClassLoaders can lead to issues such as ClassCastException and linkage errors. It is important to understand the ClassLoader hierarchy and ensure that the correct ClassLoader is used to load a class.

3. Is it possible for equals() to return false, even if the contents of two Objects are the same?

Yes, it is possible for equals() to return false, even if the contents of two Objects are the same. This can happen if the equals() method is not properly implemented in the class of the objects being compared. By default, the equals() method checks for object equality, which means that it returns true only if the two object references are pointing to the same object in memory. However, if the equals() method is overridden to compare the contents of the objects, it is important to make sure that it follows the contract for equals(), which includes being reflexive, symmetric, transitive, and consistent. If any of these conditions are not met, equals() may return false even if the contents of the objects are the same.

4. Why should compareTo() be consistent with equals() method in Java?

The compareTo() and equals() methods are both used to compare objects in Java. While the equals() method checks whether two objects are equal or not, the compareTo() method compares two objects and returns an integer value to indicate their order.

In Java, it is recommended that the compareTo() method be consistent with the equals() method. This means that if two objects are equal based on the equals() method, then their comparison using compareTo() should return a value of 0 (zero).

If the compareTo() method is not consistent with the equals() method, then it can lead to unexpected behavior in collections such as SortedSet and SortedMap. These collections rely on the ordering of objects returned by the compareTo() method. If the ordering is inconsistent with the equals() method, then it can lead to duplicate objects in the collection or objects being removed unexpectedly.

For example, consider a Person class that has name and age fields. If the compareTo() method only compares the name field, but the equals() method compares both the name and age fields, then adding a Person object to a SortedSet can lead to unexpected behavior.

Therefore, it is important to ensure that the compareTo() method is consistent with the equals() method in order to avoid unexpected behavior in collections that rely on object ordering.

5. When do Double and BigDecimal give different answers for equals() and compareTo() == 0?

Double and BigDecimal can give different answers for equals() and compareTo() == 0 when dealing with decimal values that cannot be represented exactly in binary format. For example, the value of 0.1 cannot be represented exactly in binary format, and so there is a possibility of loss of precision when performing arithmetic operations on it.

In the case of Double, the value is stored in binary format using a fixed number of bits. This can result in rounding errors and inaccuracies when performing arithmetic operations. When comparing two Double values using equals() or compareTo() == 0, these inaccuracies can result in a false comparison.

In the case of BigDecimal, the value is stored using a decimal representation, which allows for greater precision when performing arithmetic operations. However, it is still possible for inaccuracies to occur when performing arithmetic operations on values that cannot be represented exactly in decimal format. When comparing two BigDecimal values using equals() or compareTo() == 0, it is important to use the compareTo() method with a tolerance value to account for any small differences in the values.

6. How does "happens before" work in Java Memory Model?

In Java, "happens before" is a concept in the Java Memory Model (JMM) that defines the order of execution of instructions and their effects on memory. The "happens before" relationship ensures that memory writes made by one thread are visible to other threads in the correct order.

In the JMM, "happens before" is defined by a set of rules. These rules include:

Program order rule: Each action in a thread happens before every action in that thread that comes later in the program order.

Monitor lock rule: An unlock on a monitor happens before every subsequent lock on that same monitor.

Volatile variable rule: A write to a volatile field happens before every subsequent read of that same field.

Thread start rule: The start of a thread happens before any action in the started thread.

Thread join rule: All actions in a thread happen before any other thread successfully returns from a join on that thread.

Understanding the "happens before" relationship is important in ensuring that concurrent programs work correctly and consistently. It can help prevent issues such as race conditions and memory inconsistencies.

7. Why is 0.1 * 3 != 0.3 in Java?

In Java, the double data type represents decimal values as binary fractions. However, not all decimal values can be represented precisely in binary. This can lead to rounding errors when performing calculations involving decimal values.

In the case of 0.1 * 3, the decimal value 0.1 cannot be represented precisely in binary, and so it is rounded to the nearest representable binary fraction. This rounded value is then multiplied by 3, leading to a small rounding error in the result.

When this result is compared to the exact decimal value 0.3, the comparison returns false due to the small rounding error in the calculated value. This is why 0.1 * 3 != 0.3 in Java.

8. Why is (Integer) 1 == (Integer) 1 but (Integer) 222 != (Integer) 222, and which command arguments change this?

In Java, for integer values between -128 and 127, the JVM caches these values and returns the same object reference when autoboxing is used. This means that two Integer objects containing the same value will be equal only if their values are within this range.

So, when we compare two Integer objects that have values between -128 and 127, they will return true for both == and equals() methods. However, for values outside of this range, the == operator will return false even if the values are the same, because the objects are different.

This behavior can be changed by passing the JVM argument -XX:AutoBoxCacheMax=size where size is the maximum integer value that will be cached. If this value is set to 0, then no integers will be cached, and every time we use autoboxing, a new object will be created. In this case, (Integer) 1 == (Integer) 1 will be false.

9. What happens when an exception is thrown by a Thread?

When an exception is thrown by a Thread in Java, the Thread stops executing the current code and looks for an exception handler to process the exception. If the Thread does not find a handler, the Thread terminates, and the Java Virtual Machine (JVM) prints a stack trace of the exception to the console.

If the Thread is part of a multi-threaded application, the other Threads in the application continue to execute unless the exception was a fatal error that caused the JVM to terminate. In that case, all the Threads in the application are terminated, and the JVM prints a stack trace of the exception to the console.

To handle exceptions thrown by a Thread, the application can use try-catch blocks or an UncaughtExceptionHandler. The try-catch blocks can be used to catch exceptions within the Thread's run() method, while the UncaughtExceptionHandler can be used to catch exceptions that are not caught by a try-catch block.

10. What is the difference between notify() and notifyAll() calls?

In Java, notify() and notifyAll() are methods used to wake up threads that are waiting for a particular monitor. The main difference between these two methods is in the number of threads that they wake up.

When notify() is called, it wakes up only one thread that is waiting for the monitor. The thread that is woken up is not specified and is chosen by the Java Virtual Machine.

On the other hand, when notifyAll() is called, it wakes up all the threads that are waiting for the monitor. This ensures that all threads that are waiting for the monitor are notified and can resume execution.

In general, notifyAll() is preferred over notify() as it is more reliable and ensures that all threads waiting for the monitor are notified. However, notify()

can be used in situations where waking up only one thread is sufficient and can lead to better performance

11. What is the difference between System.exit() and System.halt() method?

The System.exit() method in Java terminates the currently running JVM, while the System.halt() method immediately terminates the JVM without running any shutdown hooks. The exit() method can be used to initiate a graceful shutdown of the JVM, allowing the running threads to complete their execution before terminating. On the other hand, the halt() method is used to terminate the JVM abruptly, without giving the running threads a chance to clean up their resources.

Another important difference is that System.exit() returns an exit status code to the operating system, while System.halt() does not. The exit status code can be used by the calling process or shell script to determine whether the JVM terminated normally or abnormally.

In summary, System.exit() initiates a graceful shutdown of the JVM, allowing threads to complete their execution, and returns an exit status code to the operating system. On the other hand, System.halt() abruptly terminates the JVM without running any shutdown hooks and does not return any exit status code.

12. Does following code legal in Java? Is it an example of method overloading or overriding?

```
public String getDescription(Object obj){
  return obj.toString;
}
public String getDescription(String obj){
  return obj;
}
```

And

```
public void getDescription(String obj){
    return obj;
}
```

The first two methods are an example of method overloading in Java because they have the same method name but different parameter types. The third method, however, is not valid Java syntax because it has a return type of **void** but also attempts to return a value. It should be modified to **public void getDescription(String obj) { System.out.println(obj); }** to properly print the input **String**.

This was my list of Some of the most common tricky questions in Java. It's not a bad idea to prepare a tricky Java question before appearing for any core Java interview. One or two open-ended or tricky questions are quite common in Java interviews.

CHAPTER 15:
TECHNICAL CORE JAVA INTERVIEW QUESTIONS

W hen the experience of a Java Programmer grows in the years, e.g., when it goes from beginner years (2 to 4) to more experience or sort of senior level (5 to 7 years), *Core Java Interview Questions* also change a bit. Of course, basics like **data structure, algorithms,** and **object-oriented programming** remain the same, but the types of questions will become more advanced, and their answers will definitely need to be more detailed and accurate. I often receive queries about core Java questions asked by a senior developer with 5 to 6-year experience, or, sometimes, I am going for an interview with a senior Java developer what kind of questions I should expect.

This sometimes puzzles me that once you become a senior, you automatically start taking part in the interview, and you should have an idea of what to expect in Interviews, but at the same time, I can understand that having an idea of questions before going on Interview, helps preparation.

Of course, you are not going to get a question like the one you have faced on 2 to 3 years level Java Interviews, but It also depends on different rounds of Interviews.

I have not seen many changes in the questions asked on the telephone round, which almost remains the same. You will find some fact-based, some coding questions, and a few tricky questions. On the other hand, face-to-face interviews have become more detailed and more tricky, especially with nasty follow-ups.

In this article, I am going to share some **15 technical core Java Interview Questions**, which I have seen asked by senior and experienced developers of 4 to 6 years of experience in different interviews, mostly on telephonic rounds. I am not posting answers as of now, but you can find answers to most of the questions here or on the **Javarevisited blog**.

It also covers knowledge of other JVM languages like Scala and Groovy and other platforms like Android. A perfect companion to do well in Java interviews.

15 Core Java Questions For 5 to 6 Years Experienced

All these questions have been collected from quite senior developers who have at least five years of experience. They have seen these questions on different rounds of their core Java interviews, including telephonic and face-to-face rounds on different companies, mostly on Investment banks like Barclays, Morgan, RBS, and others.

Question 1

What is Busy Spinning? Why Should You Use It in Java?

One of the interesting multithreading questions senior Java programmers are busy spinning is a *waiting strategy*, in which a thread just waits in a loop without releasing the CPU to go to sleep. This is a very advanced and specialized waiting strategy used in high-frequency trading applications when the wait time between two messages is very minimal.

By not releasing the CPU or suspending the thread, your thread retains all the cached data and instructions, which may be lost if the thread was suspended and resumed back in a different core of the CPU.

This question is quite popular in the high-frequency, low-latency programming domain, where programmers are trying for extremely low latency in the range of micro to milliseconds.

Question 2

What is Read-Write Lock? Does `ConcurrentHashMap` in Java Use the ReadWrite Lock?

ReadWrite Lock is an implementation of a *lock stripping* technique where two separate locks are used for reading and writing operations. Since the read operation doesn't modify the state of the object, it's safe to allow multiple thread access to a shared object for reading without locking, and by splitting one lock into the read and write lock, you can easily do that.

Java provides an implementation of a read-write lock in the form of the `ReentrantReadWritLock` class in the java.util.concurrent.lock package. This is worth looking at before you decide to write your own read-write locking implementation.

Also, the current implementation of `java.util.ConcurrentHashMap` doesn't use the `ReadWriteLock`; instead, it divides the Map into several segments and locks them separately using different locks. This means any given time, *only a portion of the* `ConcurrentHashMap` *is locked*, instead of the whole Map.

This core Java question is also very popular in senior and more experienced level Java interviews, e.g., 4 to 6 years, where you expect the Interviewer to go into more detail, like by asking you to provide an implementation of the read-write lock with different policies.

Question 3

How to Make an Object Immutable in Java? Why Should You Make an Object Immutable?

Well, Immutability offers several advantages, including thread safety ability to cache and result in a more readable multithreading code. Once again, this question can also go into more detail and, depending on your answer, can bring several other questions, e.g., when you mention Spring is Immutable, be ready with some reasons Why String is Immutable in Java.

Question 4

Which Design Patterns have You Used in Your Java Project?

Always expect some design patterns-related questions for the Core Java Interview for the senior developer position. It's a better strategy to mention any GOF design pattern rather than Singleton or MVC, which almost every Java developer uses.

Your best bet can be a Decorator pattern or maybe a Dependency Injection Pattern, which is quite popular in the Spring Framework. It's also good to mention only the design patterns which you have used in your project and know their tradeoffs.

It's common that once you mention a particular design pattern, say Factory or Abstract Factory, Interviewer's next question would be, *have you used this pattern in your project?* So be ready with proper examples and explain why you choose a particular pattern.

Question 5

Do you know about Open Closed Design Principle or Liskov Substitution Principle?

Design patterns are based on object-oriented design principles. I strongly feel every object-oriented developer and programmer should know, or at least have

a basic idea of, these principles and how they help you write better object-oriented code. I

Suppose you don't know the answer to this question. In that case, you can politely say No, as it's not expected from you to know the answer to every question, but by answering this question, you can make your claim stronger, as many experienced developers fail to answer basic questions like this.

Question 6

Which Design Pattern Will You Use to Shield Your Code From a Third Party library? Which Another Will Likely replace in a Couple of Months?

This is just one example of the scenario-based design pattern interview question. To test the practical experience of Java developers with more than five years of experience, companies ask this kind of question.

You can expect more real-world design problems in different formats, some with more detailed explanations with the context or some with only intent around.

One way to shield your code from a third-party library is to code against an interface rather than implementation and then use dependency injection to provide a particular implementation. This kind of question is also asked quite frequently by experienced and senior *Java developers with 5 to 7 years of experience.*

Question 7

How do you prevent SQL Injection in Java Code?

This question is asked more by J2EE and Java EE developers than core Java developers, but it is still a good question to check the JDBC and Security skill of experienced Java programmers.

You can use PreparedStatement to avoid SQL injection in Java code. Use of the `PreparedStatement` for executing SQL queries not only provides better performance but also shields your Java and J2EE application from SQL Injection attacks.

On a similar note, If you are working more on Java EE or J2EE side, then you should also be familiar with other security issues, including *Session Fixation attacks* or *Cross-Site Scripting* attacks, and how to resolve them. These are some fields and questions where a good answer can make a lot of difference in your selection.

Question 8

Tell me about different Reference types available in Java, e.g., WeakReference, SoftReference, or PhantomReference? and Why should you use them?

Well, they are different reference types coming from `java.lang.ref` package and provided to assist Java Garbage Collector in case of low memory issues. If you wrap an object with WeakReference, then it will be eligible for garbage collected if there are o strong references. They can later be reclaimed by the Garbage collector if JVM is running low on memory.

The `java.util.WeakHashMap` is a special Map implementation whose keys are the object of WeakReference, so if only Map contains the reference of any object and no other, those objects can be garbage collected if GC needs memory.

Question 9

How does the get method of HashMap work in Java?

Yes, this is still one of the most popular core Java questions for senior developer interviews. You can also expect this question on a telephonic round, followed by lots of follow-up questions.

The short answer to this question is that HashMap is based upon hash table data structure and uses the hashCode() method to calculate hash code to find the bucket location on the underlying array and the equals() method to search the object in the same bucket in case of a collision.

Question 10

Which Two Methods HashMap key Object Should Implement?

This is one of the follow-up questions I was talking about in the previous questions. Since the working of HashMap is based upon hash table data structure, any object which you want to use as a key for HashMap or any other hash-based collection, e.g., Hashtable or ConcurrentHashMap must implement equals() and hashCode() method.

The hashCode() is used to find the bucket location, i.e., the index of the underlying array, and the equals() method is used to find the right object in a linked list stored in the bucket in case of a collision.

By the way, from Java 8, HashMap also started using a tree data structure to store the object in case of a collision to reduce the worst-case performance of HashMap from O(n) to O(logN).

Question 11

Why Should an Object Used As the Key should be Immutable?

This is another follow-up to the previous core Java interview questions. It's good to test the depth of technical knowledge of candidates by asking more and more questions on the same topic. If you know about Immutability, you can answer this question by yourself.

The short answer to this question is key should be immutable, so that hashCode() method always returns the same value.

Since the hash code returned by the `hashCode(,)` method depends on the content of the object, i.e., values of member variables. If an object is mutable, then those values can change, and so is the hash code. If the same object returns a different hash code once you insert the value in HashMap, you will end up searching in different bucket locations and will not be able to retrieve the object.

That's why the key objective should be immutable. It's not a rule enforced by the compiler, but you should take care of it as an experienced programmer.

Question 12

How does `ConcurrentHashMap` achieve its Scalability?

Sometimes this multithreading + collection interview question is also asked as the difference between `ConcurrentHashMap` and Hashtable in Java. The problem with synchronized HashMap or Hashtable was that the whole Map is locked when a thread performs any operation with Map.

The `java.util.ConcurrentHashMap` class solves this problem by using a *lock stripping* technique, where the whole map is locked at different segments, and only a particular segment is locked during the write operation, not the whole map.

The `ConcurrentHashMap` also achieves its scalability by allowing lock-free reads as read is a thread-safe operation.

Question 13

How do you share an object between threads? Or How to pass an object from one thread to another?

There are multiple ways to do that, like Queues, Exchanger, etc., but `BlockingQueue` using the Producer-Consumer pattern is the easiest way to pass an object from one thread to another.

Question 14

How do you find out if your program has a deadlock?

By taking thread dump using kill -3, using JConsole or VisualVM), I suggest preparing this core java interview question in more detail, as the Interviewer definitely likes to go with more detail, e.g., they will press with questions like, have you really done that in your project or not?

Question 15

How do you avoid deadlock while coding?

By ensuring locks are acquired and released in an ordered manner.

That's all on this list of *Core Java Interview Questions for senior developers and experienced programmers. You can go through all these chapters and quickly revise all Java concept based questions before your interview.*

CONCLUSION

In this book, we have covered some of the most common and important technical core Java interview questions that you are likely to encounter. We started with the basics of object-oriented programming and Java syntax, then moved on to more advanced topics such as class loaders, enums, strings, and collections.

We also covered important Java concepts such as inheritance, abstract classes, and interfaces, as well as essential Java APIs for working with dates and times, web services, and network programming. By understanding these topics deeply, you will be better prepared to ace your Java technical interviews and build robust Java applications that meet the demands of modern software development.

Remember, technical interviews can be challenging, but with practice and preparation, you can increase your chances of success. Make sure to review these concepts and practice coding problems to build your skills and confidence. And always be open to learning and improving your knowledge of Java and software development in general. Good luck on your journey of grokking the Java interview!

www.ingramcontent.com/pod-product-compliance
Lightning Source LLC
LaVergne TN
LVHW051735050326
832903LV00023B/924